Title: **Let My People Go**
Format: **Poster**
Art Director/Designer:
Dan Reisinger
Client: **No client**
Country: **Israel**
Year: **1969**

By adapting the communist hammer and sickle, this poster opposes the Soviet policy prohibiting the immigration of Jews from the USSR. *(top left)*

Title: **Again?**
Format: **Poster**
Art Director/Designer:
Dan Reisinger
Client: **No client**
Country: **Israel**
Year: **1993**

A prescient 1993 warning against the resurgence of fascistic and anti-Semitic movements in the formerly communist countries of Eastern Europe is the message of this bold and dynamic poster. *(top right)*

Title: **Diskurs Macht hegemonie**
Format: **Magazine cover**
Art Director/Designer:
Rico Lins
Client: **Germinal Verlag, Bochum/Klartext Verlag, Bochum**
Country: **Brazil**
Year: **1988**

This image for the German political magazine *KulturRevolution* is a collaged composite, a Mr. Potato Head, if you will, of four left-wing icons, Mao Tse Tung, Karl Marx, Leon Trotsky, and Michel Foucault, symbolizing an attempt to combine various ideologies in hopes of creating something stronger, when, in fact, the result does not work. *(bottom)*

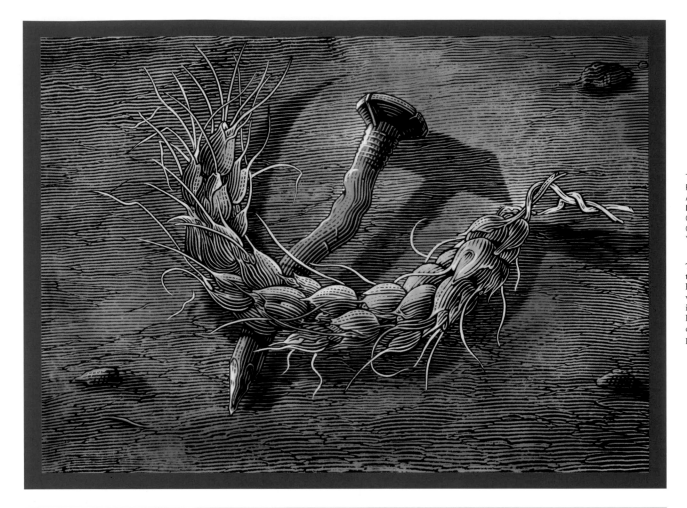

Title: **Nail and Wheat**
Format: **Poster**
Art Director/Designer:
Istvan Orosz
Client: **No client**
Country: **Hungary**
Year: **1989**

The careful placement of the nail (hit with the hammer) and sheath of wheat (cut with the sickle) in the position of the Soviet hammer and sickle symbol convey the victimization of people under communism.

Title: **Concert Poster**
Format: **Poster**
Art Director/Designer:
Istvan Orosz
Client: **No client**
Country: **Hungary**
Year: **1990**

This bold and immediate poster advertises a Budapest concert for the victims of communism.

Title: **Comrades, It's Over**
Format: **Poster**
Art Director/Designer:
Istvan Orosz
Client: **M.D.F.**
Country: **Hungary**
Year: **1989**

This work was created by
a designer/illustrator who
grew up in, and spent his
life in, Soviet-dominated
Hungary. He was surprised
and delighted in 1989 when
he drew this poster and
soon afterward, the Soviet
Army returned home.

Title: **Poster to Commemorate the Day of Yugoslav Youth**
Format: **Poster**
Art Director/Designer: **New Collectivism**
Client: **Socialist Youth League of Slovenia**
Country: **Slovenia**
Year: **1987**

This prize-winning poster celebrating Marshall Josip Broz Tito's birthday is a redesign of a 1930's Richard Klein poster (*below*). NSK (Neue Slowenische Kunst) believes the traumas of the past affecting the present and the future can be healed only by returning to the initial conflicts. NSK narrowly escaped imprisonment when the original Nazi source became public knowledge.

aTitle: **Exterior of the NSK State Berlin**
Format: **Exterior design**
Art Director/Designer: **New Collectivism**
Client: **Volksbuhne Theater**
Country: **Slovenia**
Year: **1993**

NSK hosted a show at the Volksbuhne theater in the historical center of Berlin, once among the most prominent theater establishments of the twentieth century. During the show, the Volksbuhne was declared a territory of the NSK State and entry was only permitted to NSK passport holders with valid visas. However, a "consulate office" was open non-stop issuing information and documents to potential NSK citizens interested in entering. *(top)*

Title: **NSK Headquarters**
Format: **Photograph**
Art Director/Designer: **New Collectivism**
Client: **NSK Information Center**
Country: **Slovenia**
Year: **1999**

Shown here is the NSK state information office. The passport division is placed in front of a wall mounted with photographs of various NSK artifacts. *(bottom left)*

Title: **The State of NSK**
Format: **Poster**
Art Director/Designer: **New Collectivism**
Client: **NSK**
Country: **Slovenia**
Year: **1994**

New Collectivism is an independent graphic design collective and a member of the NSK organization. In this poster, the Utopian goal is expressed by NSK as a state. This poster was used to promote various NSK events. *(bottom right)*

Title: **NSK Merchandise**
Format: **Book cover**
Art Director/Designer:
New Collectivism
Client: **No client**
Country: **Slovenia**
Year: **1999**

The back cover of the NSK catalog/monograph shows NSK merchandise designed for an exhibition at the Museum of Modern Art in Ljubljana. The transition from socialism to capitalism and the creation of European monetary union in 1999 is represented by the number 99 shown throughout. All products featured are for sale.

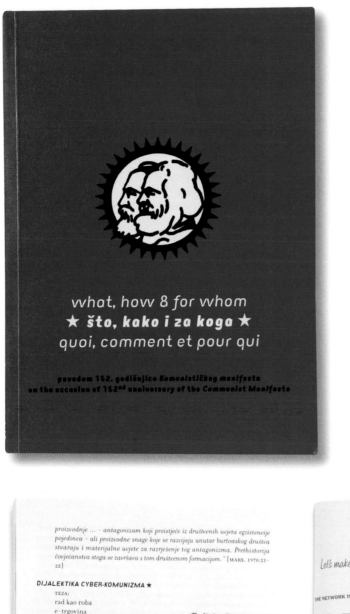

Title: What, how & for
whom—152nd anniversary
of the Communist
Manifesto
Format: **Book/Catalogue**
Art Director/Designer:
Dejan Kršić
Client: **What, how & for
whom (WHW)**
Country: **Croatia**
Year: **2003**

The dynamic cover of this
152nd Anniversary edition
of the *The Communist
Manifesto* boldly features
Karl Marx and Friedrich
Engles. The book serves as
a catalog to an exhibition
and various events held in
Croatia that were re-staged
the following year in
Austria. The publication
contains essays by several
famous theoreticians and
writers, and is distributed
in bookshops, galleries, and
museums.

1er EXPO en FRANCE de PÉTER PÓCS

MAIRIE DE CASTELMORON DU 6 AU 28 AOÛT TOUS LES APRÉS-MIDI

L'AFFICHE À CASTELMORON D'ALBRET

Title: **Péter Pócs's First Exhibition in France**
Format: **Poster**
Art Director/Designer: **Péter Pócs**
Client: **Unknown**
Country: **Hungary**
Year: **1988**

This poster was originally designed for an exhibition of Hungarian artists at the eighth Venice Biennial. It was rejected as ideologically inappropriate due to its portrayal of the communist symbols, but was later used as a poster for Péter Pócs's own exhibition in Paris.

Title: **1989**
Format: **Poster**
Art Director/Designer:
Péter Pócs
Client: **No client**
Country: **Hungary**
Year: 1989

This self printed poster for the SZDSZ (Union of the Free Democrats) was considered too strong to be used. The bold graphic depicts the destruction of communism and the dates in the corner refer to the Hungarian Freedom Flight (October 23, 1956) and the eventual collapse of communism in 1989.

Title: **301**
Format: **Poster**
Art Director/Designer:
Péter Pócs
Client: **Union of the Free Democrats**
Country: **Hungary**
Year: **1989**

Russian troops crushed the 1956 Hungarian Revolution, killing many Hungarian citizens and burying them in mass graves. One of the graves, in which the revolutionary leader Imre Nagy is buried, was marked with the number 301. The blood on this poster is in the shape of Hungary.

Title: **Simile**
Format: **Poster**
Art Director/Designer:
Péter Pócs
Client: **Peter Stefanovits**
Country: **Hungary**
Year: **1988**

This poster, created for an
exhibition of graphic
designer Peter Stefanovits's
work, was shown on
Hungarian prime-time
news. The news censored
the controversial image of
the communist star
attached to the cross and
showed only the text at the
bottom.

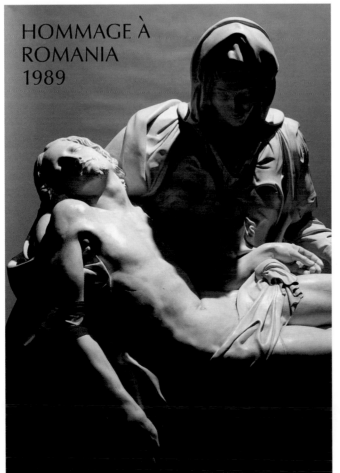

Title: **Hommage à
Romania 1989**
Format: **Poster**
Art Director/Designer:
Péter Pócs
Client: **No client**
Country: **Hungary**
Year: **1989**

The famous phrase from
the 1960s, "The revolution
will be televised," became a
reality in 1989. As a result,
there was an immediate
reaction around the world,
and this poster, a response
to the Romanian revolu-
tion, was already printing
on the third day of the
bloody event.

ISRAELI LAW ENFORCEMENT

Since the outbreak of the Intifada in September 2000, approximately 48% of Palestinians killed by Israeli soldiers were males between the ages 19-29; this equates to more than 1320 men. Approximately 61% of all deaths were a result of live ammunition in response to stone-throwing.

Title: **Israeli Law Enforcement**
Format: **Poster**
Art Director/Designer: **Rebecca Rapp**
Client: **"Don't Say You Didn't Know" exhibition curated by Dana Bartelt**
Country: **USA**
Year: **2003**

The designer, an activist for the International Solidarity Movement, illustrates the current situation in Palestine with this powerful image. The design combined the well-known *Pieta* (a symbol for the slain) with a reference to Jesus (who was shown no mercy) to illustrate how history is repeating itself with the slaying of young, innocent Palestinian men. The designer did not intend to make this a religious piece and noted that if another well-known figure had suffered similar treatment, he or she would have been an equally appropriate analogy.

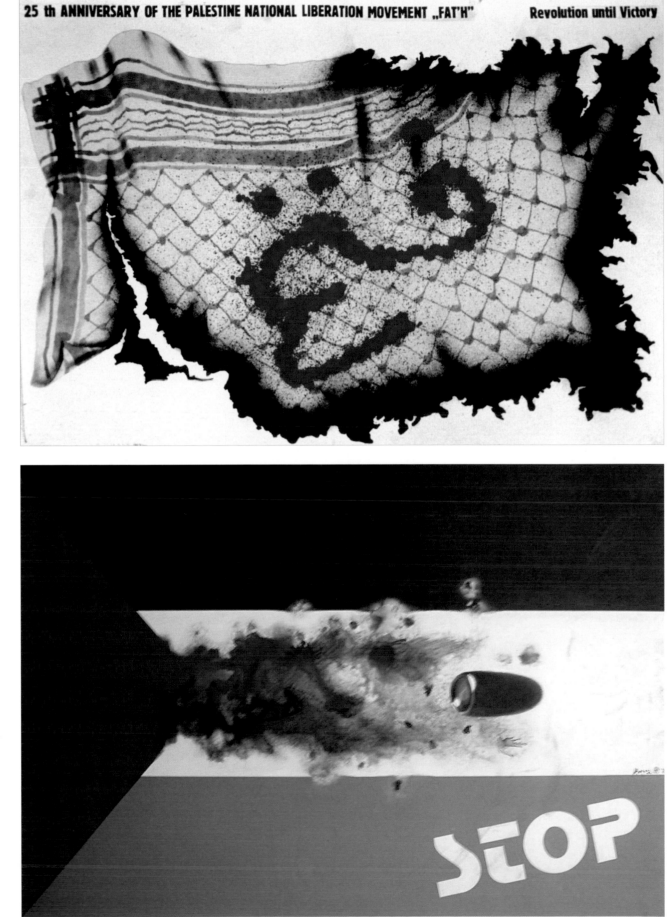

25 th ANNIVERSARY OF THE PALESTINE NATIONAL LIBERATION MOVEMENT „FAT'H" **Revolution until Victory**

Title: **Revolution until Victory**
Format: **Poster**
Art Director/Designer: **Unknown**
Client: **No client**
Country: **Poland**
Year: **1989**

The war-torn kaffiyah has the word Fateh in Arabic "blood" red lettering. The kaffiyah was turned into a symbol of the Palestinian state by Yassir Arafat and also became a symbol of the Fedayeen (Palestinian Freedom Fighters).

Title: **Stop**
Format: **Poster**
Art Director/Designer: **Unknown Polish artist, from the collection of Dana Bartelt**
Client: **PLO (Palestine Liberation Organization)**
Country: **Unknown**
Year: **1980s**

In this poster, another one in a series created by Polish artists in solidarity with the Palestinian cause, the Palestine flag is shown pierced by an Israeli sniper's bullet.

STOP

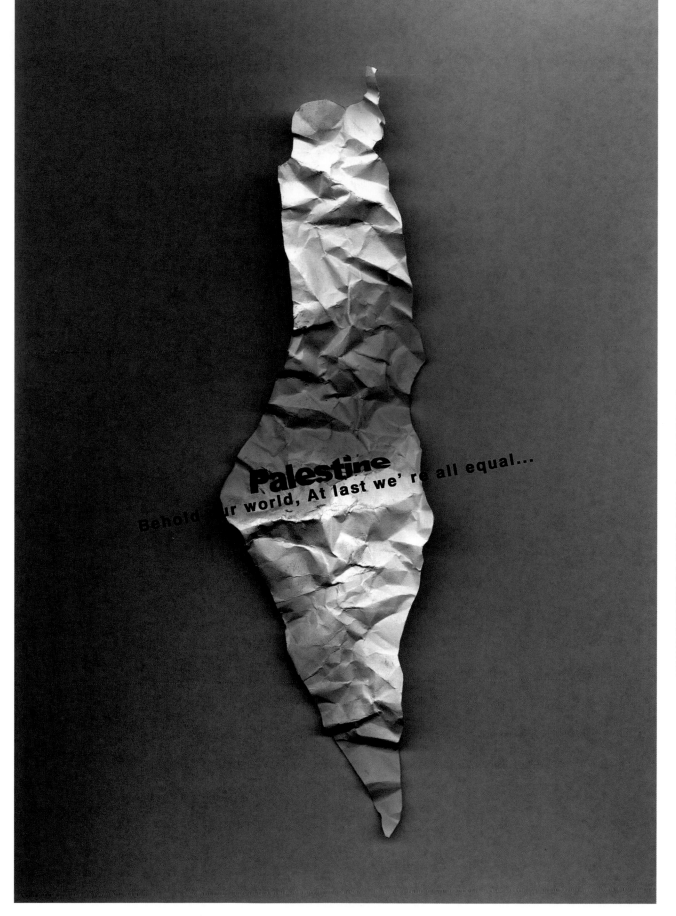

Title: **Palestine**
Format: **Poster**
Art Director/Designer:
Pedram Harby
Client: **No client**
Country: **Iran**
Year: **2004**

The copy line for this poster supporting the Palestinian position states: "Behold our world, At last we're all equal..." The image of a discarded map brought out of the waste basket in an effort "to iron out the creases and restore it to its original place" is persuasive. The designer's idea was to "display the crumpled map of Palestine in the void of indifference that surrounds it." This poster was designed to take part in the 9th triennial of political posters in Mons, Belgium.

e.qual (êl'kwêl) adj. [Lat. aequalis < aequus, even.] 1. Having the same measure, quantity, or value as another. 2. Math. Being the same or identical to in value. 3 a. Having the same rights, privileges, or status <equal in accord of law> b. Being the same for all members of a group <gave every employee an equal chance> 4 a. Having the qualities, as strength, intelligence, or ability needed for a situation or task. b. Sufficient in extent, amount, or degree. — n. One equal to another. — vt. e.qua.led, e.qua.ling, e.quals or e.qualled, e.qualling, e.quals 1. To be equal to, esp. in value. 2. To do or produce something equal to.

Sharing Jerusalem: Two Capitals for Two States

Title: Equal
Format: Poster
Art Director/Designer:
Bülent Erkmen
Client: Bat Shalom, Israel
Country: Turkey
Year: 1998

The impossibility of achieving agreement on the mere definition of the word *equal* makes a powerful graphic statement in this poster for the Sharing Jerusalem: Two Capitals project.

Title: Art Against the Wall
Format: Mural
Art Director/Designers:
Eric Drooker,
Palestinian children
Client: No client
Country: Palestine
Year: 2004

The Israeli government calls it "the security barrier." Palestinians call it "the apartheid wall." Twice as tall as the Berlin Wall, its projected span is 500 miles (805 kilometers). The artist calls it "the greatest blank canvas in the world." He painted this mural with the help of local children in the occupied West Bank village of Masha.

Title: Palestine Is
our Home / Stop Israeli
Brutality Racism Against
Palestinians / End the
Occupation of Palestine
Now
Format: Posters
Art Director/Designer:
Samia A. Halaby
Client: No client
Country: USA
Year: 1991

The black background and
bright colors in *End the
Occupation of Palestine
Now* and *Palestine Is our
Home* are a deliberate
homage to Palestinian
Libertarian art of the 1970s
and 1980s and appeal to
the visual requirements of
news photographers.
These posters were used in
Washington, D.C. as protest
against the first Gulf War
in 1991.

*Stop Israeli Brutality
Racism Against Palestinians*
was created to hang in the
artist's home to identify her
political and ethnic
background to visitors. The
artist noted that she "did
not want to waste time
with those who hated my
national background . . . ."

Title: **Stone Throwing Boy**
Format: **Poster**
Art Director/Designer:
**Unknown, from the
collection of Dana Bartelt**
Client: **PLO (Palestine
Liberation Organization)**
Country: **Palestine**
Year: **2000**

The Israeli tank is unseen
in this famous photograph
of a Palestinian boy
throwing stones. This
poster was given away by
the Palestinian Liberation
Organization office in
Ramallah during the
second Intifada of 2000.

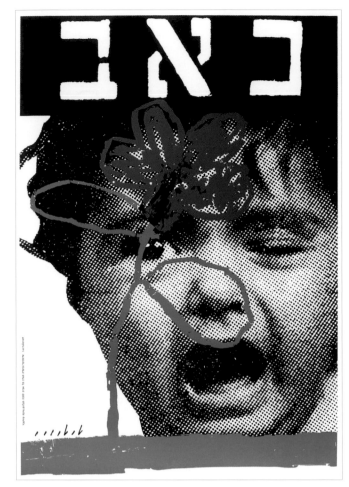

Title: **Pain**
Format: **Poster**
Art Director/Designer:
David Tartakover
Photographer:
Micha Kirshner
Client: **No client**
Country: **Israel**
Year: **1989**

It's almost impossible to imagine how difficult life as an Israeli designer critical of Israeli military behavior must be. Nevertheless, voices consistently opposing the conflict and seeking resolution have emerged. This poster was created for a group of Israelis who refuse to serve their military service in the occupied territories and appeals to others to do the same through this little Palestinian girl who lost an eye to an Israeli rubber bullet. The Hebrew word for "pain" displayed prominently across the top of this poster can also mean "as a father."

Title: **Man Nature Society**
Format: **Poster**
Art Director/Designer:
David Tartakover
Photography: **Alex Levac**
Client: **No client**
Country: **Israel**
Year: **1992**

This poster, designed for the "Man Nature Society" international exhibition held in Moscow, features the colors of the Palestinian flag behind the title blocks.

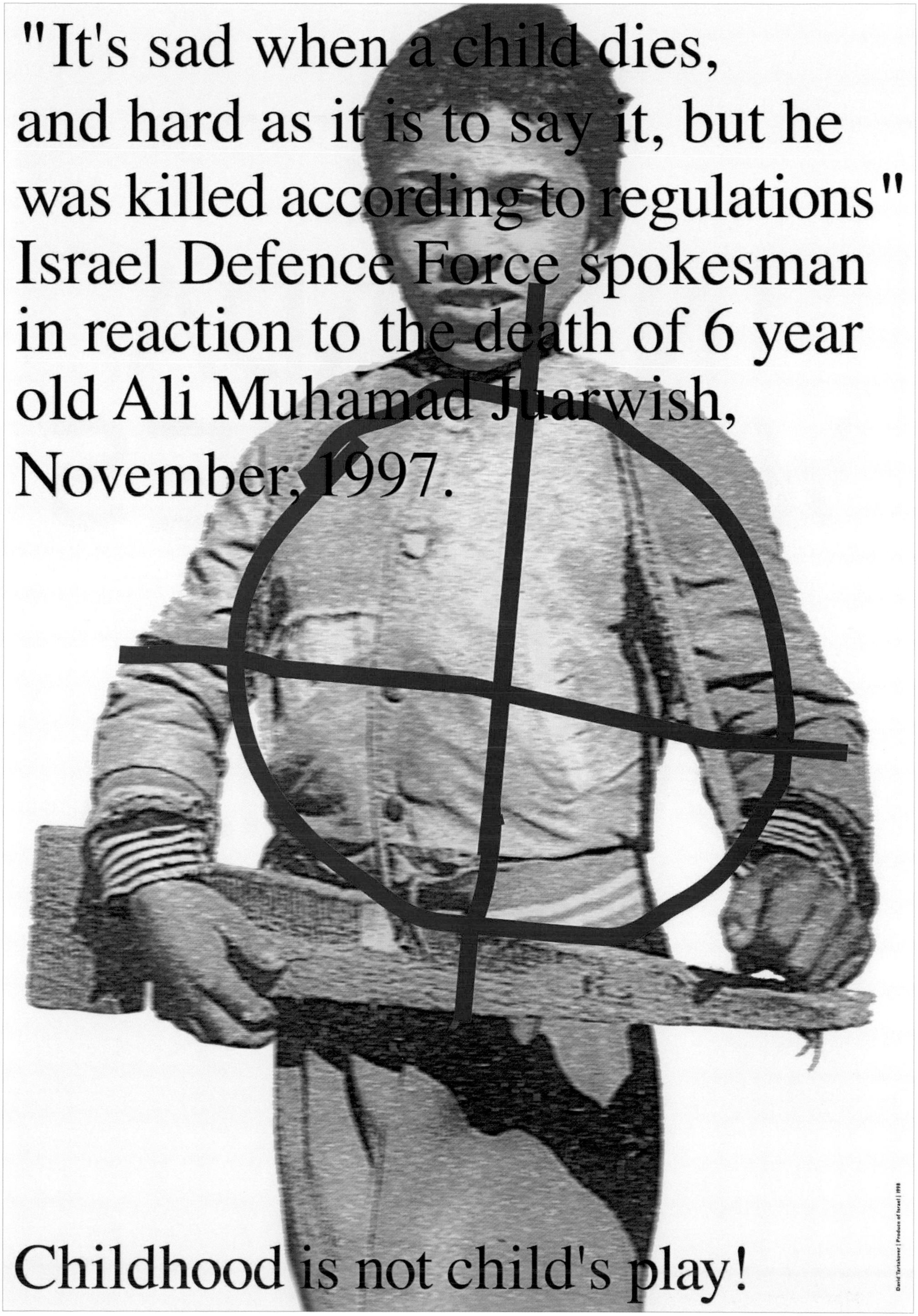

"It's sad when a child dies, and hard as it is to say it, but he was killed according to regulations" Israel Defence Force spokesman in reaction to the death of 6 year old Ali Muhamad Juarwish, November, 1997.

Childhood is not child's play!

Title: **Childhood Is Not Child's Play!**
Format: **Poster**
Art Director/Designer: **David Tartakover**
Client: **No client**
Country: **Israel**
Year: **1998**

A quote from an Israeli Defense Forces spokesman explaining that this six-year-old Palestinian boy was "killed according to regulation" offers little comfort, as it remains strikingly apparent that the child pictured here is much too young to stand in the crosshairs of a political battle.

THE INTIFADA WELCOMES THE ICOGRADA

Title: **The Intifada Welcomes the Icograda**
Format: **Poster**
Art Director/Designer:
David Tartakover
Client: **No client**
Country: **Israel**
Year: **1989**

Intifada, which literally translates to "an abrupt and sudden waking from an unconscious state," is a word that has come to symbolize the Palestinian uprising against Israeli occupation. More than 11,000 Palestinians have been injured in Intifada protests against Israel. When Icograda, the International Council of Graphic Design Associations, decided to hold its biannual congress in Tel Aviv, this poster was created to announce the conference and remind the international design community that the role of a designer varies with the political climate in which he or she operates.

13th congress of icograda international council of graphic design associations august 27-31 1989 tel aviv

Title: **Happy New Fear**
Format: **Poster**
Art Director/Designer:
David Tartakover
Photographer: **Oded Klein**
Client: **No client**
Country: **Israel**
Year: **1995**

Rather than a stylized version of a weapon, this depiction is starkly realistic. The barrel reads, "Desert Eagle .357 Magnum Pistol—Israel Military Industries," contrasting the harsh reality of Israeli occupation with the festive celebration of a new year. This poster is a reminder that, for many, time only represents a continuation of fear and violence.

Title: **Have a Year of Peace and Security**
Format: **Poster**
Art Director/Designer:
Yossi Lemel
Client: **No client**
Country: **Israel**
Year: **2002**

Irony is an important tool of dissent, but if it lapses into cleverness, the message can be compromised. In this instance, the sense of contrivance may be too evident.

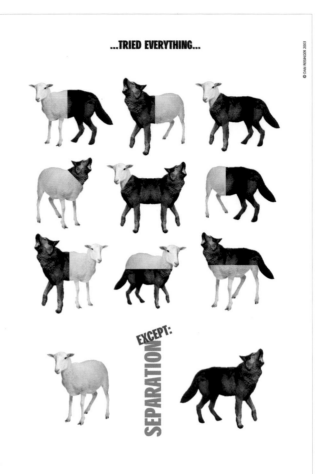

Title: **Separation**
Format: **Poster**
Art Director/Designer:
Dan Reisinger
Client: **No client**
Country: **Israel**
Year: **2003**

After many failed attempts to live in harmony, this poster supports the building of the wall in Israel: "To prevent the infiltration of suicide bombers into Israel and to terminate Israel's intervention into the everyday life of Palestinians."

Title: **F-16i**
Format: **Poster**
Art Director/Designer:
Yossi Lemel
Client: **No client**
Country: **Israel**
Year: **2000**

Critical of the Israeli Air Force, this poster sarcastically suggests that war within the region has become the natural order and the Israeli jet fighter has become another dangerous species.

Title: **Blood Bath 2002**
Format: **Poster**
Art Director/Designer:
Yossi Lemel
Client: **No client**
Country: **Israel**
Year: **2002**

This chilling image conveys
the designer's opposition to
the endless bloodshed
between Israelis and
Palestinians in which
neither side is able to wash
away responsibility for the
situation. References to
morgues and suicides are
both intentional and
disturbing.

Title: **Israel Palestine 2003**
Format: **Poster**
Art Director/Designer: **Yossi Lemel**
Client: **No client**
Country: **Israel**
Year: **2003**

The imagery in this poster references peace as a living, fragile organism, and questions why Israel's efforts to preserve it, while well intentioned, have not yielded the desired results.

Title: **Israel Palestine 2004**
Format: **Poster**
Art Director/Designer: **Yossi Lemel**
Client: **No client**
Country: **Israel**
Year: **2004**

Depicting a peace process that was brutally cut off in the middle of an attempt to achieve cooperation, this graphic image also references the graphic realities of lost limbs and body parts that are a result of this ongoing conflict.

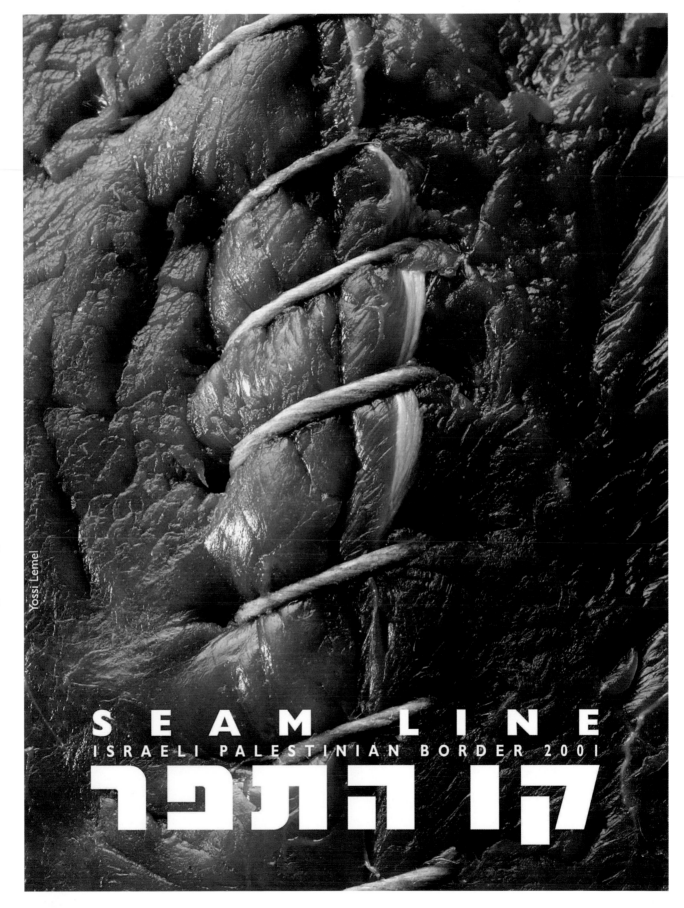

Title. **Seamline**
Format: **Poster**
Art Director/Designer:
Yossi Lemel
Client: **No client**
Country: **Israel**
Year: **2001**

Context creates meaning. This image of raw meat bound together by string could almost appear in a cookbook as an example of how to tie a roast. When placed into the context of the seamline—the border between the Israeli and Palestinian territories—the meaning darkens. The subtle color variation between the two sides intentionally and cleverly reflects the skin tones of those involved.

Yossi Lemel

SEAM LINE
ISRAELI PALESTINIAN BORDER 2001
קו התפר

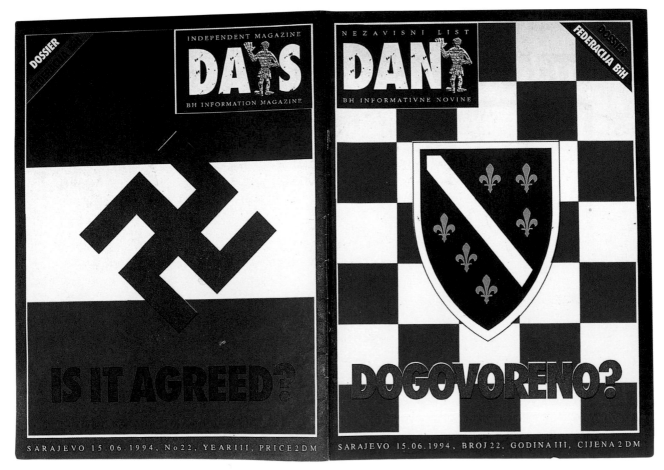

Title: *Dani* magazine
Format: **Magazine covers**
Art Director/Designer:
Trio Sarajevo
Client: *DANI* magazine
Country: **Bosnia
and Herzegovina**
Year: **1995**

DANI magazine, the political weekly considered to be the most courageous magazine in Sarajevo during the siege, consistently produced provocative covers. On this cover Radovan Karadzic, the former President of the Republica Srpska accused of the slaughter of thousands of Bosnian Muslims and Croats who has twice been indicted by the United Nations war crimes tribunal, is shown opposite Adolf Hitler indicating their similar style of "leadership."

These front and back covers of *DANI* magazine question whether the new unification into two separate states, the Bosnian Republic and the Serbian Republic, according to Dayton accord, have achieved the designed objectives.

This horrifying image depicting the results of a Serbian mortar explosion that landed near a market square is almost too much to bear. This event, and the published images from it, caused foreign governments to finally take action.

These images of Muslim families being expelled from Serbian controlled territories in Bosnia are evidence of the ethnic cleansing that took place in the mid 1990s.

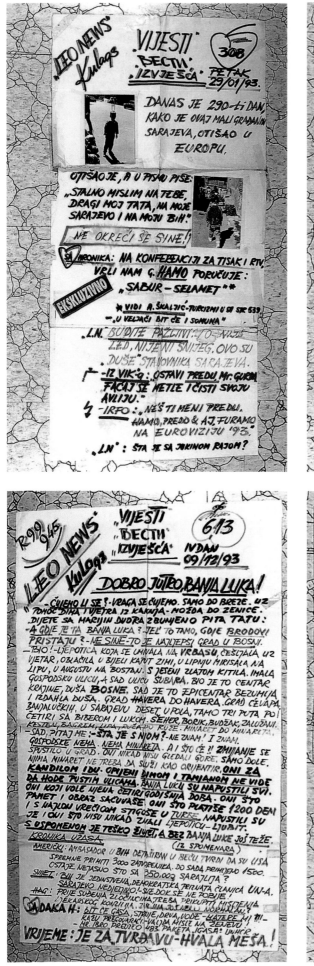

Title: *Leo News*
Format: Handwritten
posters
Art Director/Designer:
Malik "Kula" Kulenović
Client: No client
Country: Bosnia
and Herzegovina
Year: 1993-94

Numbering each edition
of this handwritten
newspaper with the day of
the siege of Sarajevo
increased the political
power of this publication
produced by a news vendor.
Each edition combined
Cyrillic and Roman
alphabets, making a
poignant plea for ethnic
unity. The use of the two
alphabets turned out to
be as significant as the
news itself.

Title: **Survival Map '92–'96**
Format: **Poster**
Art Directors/Designers:
**Suada Kapić,
Emir Kasumagić**
Illustrator: **Ozren Pavlović**
Photographer:
Drago Resner
Client:
FAMA International
Country: **Bosnia
and Herzegovina**
Year: **1996**

The romance and beauty of an old hand-drawn map of Sarajevo is appropriated by the illustrator showing us instead the tragedy of the long siege, which lasted 1,395 days—the longest in modern times. This commemorative map details the horror of being a city set snuggly in the mountains with a vast array of artillery, ready to demolish it at a moment's notice. This poster has been sold and distributed around the world and is said to be displayed at the International Criminal Tribunal office in the Hague.

Title: **The Fall of
Yugoslavia 1991-1999,
causes and consequences**
Format: **Map**
Art Directors/Designers:
**Miran Norderland,
Jelena Vranić**
Client:
FAMA International
Country: **Bosnia
and Herzegovina**
Year: **1999**

This ambitious work documents the events that occurred in the former Yugoslavia between 1991 and 1999. When the Kosovo crisis and conflict started, the designer realized the need for connecting all the events in order to explain that Kosovo was not an isolated conflict, but a consequence of the 1991–1995 wars that concluded with the Dayton Peace Accords. It has been distributed around the world as a teaching aid and a "contribution for national truth and reconciliation and democratization of the post war society."

FAMA

SARAJEVO

SURVIVAL GUIDE

SARAJEVO A UNIQUE CITY ON THE PLANET !
SARAJEVO LIVES THE POST-CATACLYSM !
SARAJEVO IS SCIENCE FICTION ! SARAJEVO
MAKES *MAD MAX 5* POSSIBLE ! SARAJEVO CAN
TEACH YOU HOW TO SURVIVE THE POST
CATACLYSM ! SARAJEVO IS THE END OF THE 21 ST
CENTURY ! SARAJEVO THE CITY OF THE FUTURE !
SARAJEVO BUILDS A NEW CIVILIZATION ON THE
RUINS OF THE OLD ONE ! SARAJEVO TEACHES !
SARAJEVO GIVES YOU INSTRUCTIONS ON HOW TO
SURVIVE !

Title: *Survival Guide*
Format: Book
Author: Suada Kapić
Designer: Boris Dogan
Client:
FAMA International
Country: Bosnia
and Herzegovina
Year: 1993

This book was created to document the survival tactics used during the siege of Sarajevo to facilitate everyday needs, such as heating buildings, making alcohol, and taking care of sick animals. The writers wanted to pass their hard-earned knowledge onto others who may one day experience similar events. Kapić was taken out of Bosnia during the siege by the Japanese government in order to promote this book. After, she returned to Bosnia, still under siege.

Non-alcoholic beverages

Or, everything tastes better than the boiled water. And, what are we going to do once all trees are gone?

Birch-juice
Young birch tree should be drilled. In the hole a few centimeters deep, one should install a tube. Leave it for forty-eight hours, while the juice is being collected in a tin. During April and May, one can get 8 liters of juice during 48 hours. Juice can be mixed with wine, sugar, yeast or lemon, and then left to ferment. This process demands several days.

Fir-tree-juice
Cut the needles of young fir-tree, and keep them in hot water for two or three minutes. Then cut them in tiny pieces, press, and put in cold water for two or three hours. If days are sunny, keep the jar in the sun. Filter and sweeten before serving. Pine-tree and juniper-tree can do just as well.

Boza
Once well known and very popular refreshment, gone out of style. Could be found only in two or three pastry-shops on Baščaršija.
0.5 kilos of corn flour
1 package of yeast
8 l of water
sugar and lemon-powder, if you have it and as you like it.
Put the corn flour in some water and leave it for 24 hours. Then cook it on a low heat about two hours, mixing occasionally and adding water. When it cools of, add the yeast and leave for 24 hours. Then add sugar and lemon-powder, leave it for three more hours and add 8 to 10 liters of water. Should be served cold.

Alcoholic beverages

Sarajevo cognac
3-4 spoons of sugar
water
ethyl alcohol
The quality of cognac depends on the brand of alcohol and on the quality of the Sarajevo water, preferably brought from some of the protected wells. Fry the sugar, add some water to melt it, and bring to a boil. Mix the water and alcohol in a ratio of 2.5:1, and add the sugar.

Wine
1/2 kilo of sugar
5 l of boiled water
1/2 kilo of rice
1 pack of yeast
10 cl of alcohol, or 20 cl of rum
Mix all the ingredients, and pour them in hermetically closed canister. Ten days later, extract the wine through a Melita coffee-filter.

Sakl
5 l of water
0.5 kilos of rice
0.5 kilos of sugaryeast
Should sit for seven days and ferment. Then filter the drink and use rice in the pie.

Medical care

Medical care: its main characteristic is very friendly personnel, which was not the case before the war. It is very efficient. Aside from the hospital and emergency rooms, you will hear quickly about all the improvised ambulances. The maternity hospital has been shelled and is out of use, so babies are born in the regular hospital. When visiting the dentist, you should take your bottle with water, and gloves, which she can use while treating you.

Pharmacies are working, but medicine is mostly missing. Bring your own vitamins. In emergency — look for the locations of Benevolencija and Caritas.

Veterinarian's Clinic

The Veterinarian's Clinic is on Daniel Ozmo Street, in the store where they used to sell hi-fi equipment. Its hours are from 9 a.m. and 2 p.m. Lines are very long, and the service is full, including very complex surgical operations. Sarajevo became the city of abandoned pedigree dogs who are sadly roaming the streets, frozen, hungry and wounded. Their owners have left Sarajevo and left them behind, or they don't have food to even feed themselves.

72   73

Cemeteries

The beauty of old Sarajevo cemeteries has been ruined by growing needs. They have been reopened when two contemporary cemeteries — Bare and Vlakovo — became inaccessible. Small old cemeteries which were active for certain neighborhoods, even streets (mahalska) were closed in 1878, with the arrival of the Austro-Hungarian Empire. More than a century later, they started functioning again. People are being buried next to the mosques, on playgrounds in front of their houses. The old military cemeteries — Austrian, of the First Yugoslavia, German, and a partisan one — are full. Since September, the small stadium in the sports complex Koševo, was turned into a cemetery, too. Funerals are held in early morning or dusk hours, to avoid the shelling. There is a rule not to go to the funerals and not to have flowers and wreaths. They cannot be bought anyway, even if someone would want to.

76   77

NO TEETH...?
A MUSTACHE...?
SMEL LIKE SHIT...?

BOSNIAN GIRL

Šejla Kamerić
Graffiti written by an unknown Dutch soldier on an army barracks wall in Potočari, Srebrenica, 1994/95.
Royal Netherlands Army troops, as part of the UN Protection Force (UNPROFOR) in Bosnia
and Herzegovina 1992–95, were responsible for protecting the Srebrenica safe area.
Photograpy by Tarik Samarah

Title: **Bosnian Girl**
Format: **Poster**
Art Director/Designer:
Šejla Kamerić
Photographer:
Tarik Samarah
Client: **No client**
Country: **Bosnia
and Herzegovina**
Year: **Graffiti: 1994/1995,
Poster: 2003**

Contemptuous graffiti
written by an unknown
soldier from the Royal
Netherlands Army troops
was found and photo-
graphed in a factory used
by the troops as a U.N.
Protection Forces barracks
during the siege of
Srebrenica (a building later
used by Serbs to execute
Bosnians.) This graffiti
clearly explains the
attitudes and failure of the
U.N. forces responsible for
protecting the safe area.
The artist positioned this
found graffiti over an image
of a Bosnian girl to
illustrate the Srebrenica
tragedy and the prejudice
Bosnians faced, as well as
the prejudice Bosnians
have toward others. The
work was a public project
and was used on posters,
billboards, magazine ads,
and postcards.

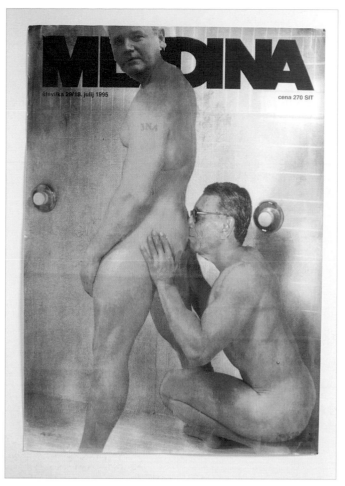

Title: *Mladina*
Format: **Magazine cover**
Art Director/Designer:
Trio Sarajevo
Client: *Mladina* **magazine**
Country: **Slovenia**
Year: **1995**

A collaged image showing
UN Secretary-General
Boutros Boutros Galli
kissing the lower back side
of the Yugoslav-Serbian
President Slobodon
Milosevic was featured on
the cover of *Mladina*
magazine because the
United Nations did not
want to take a strong stand
on the Yugoslavian-Serbian
atrocities in Bosnia.

Title: **UNable**
Format: **Poster**
Art Director/Designer:
Yossi Lemel
Client: **No client**
Country: **Israel**
Year: **1995**

In this political poster, the
artist chose a helpless,
impotent turtle on its back
to symbolize the United
Nations (UN), after its ineffective attempt to resolve
conflict in Bosnia.

ASSOCIATION FOR SAVING HUMANS

Title: **Made in Bosnia**
Format: **Poster**
Art Director/Designer:
Anur Hadziomerspahić
Client: **No client**
Country: **Bosnia
and Hertzegovina**
Year: **1998**

The numerous European
campaigns protesting the
killing of animals incited
this campaign against the
killing of humans in Bosnia.

Title: **Bosnian Postcards**
Format: **Postcard**
Art Director/Designer:
Anur Hadziomerspahić
Client: **No client**
Country: **Bosnia
and Hertzegovina**
Year: **1998**

This postcard (*right*) reflects the three ethnic and religious groups (Serbs, Croats, Muslims) that are fighting together as one army. By showing their private parts, they are showing their ethnic diversity. Because Muslims are the only group that circumcise their men, in the past conflicts this has been a way of identifying them.

After the war, a portion of the population turned toward faith in a more aggressive and expressive manner than they had in the recent past.

Title: **Sarajevo Humor**
Format: **Poster**
Art Director/Designer:
Anur Hadziomerspahić
Client: **No client**
Country: **Bosnia
and Hertzegovina**
Year: **1998**

Tens of thousands of limbs have been destroyed by landmines. As a result, Bosnia is currently the world champion in sitting volleyball.

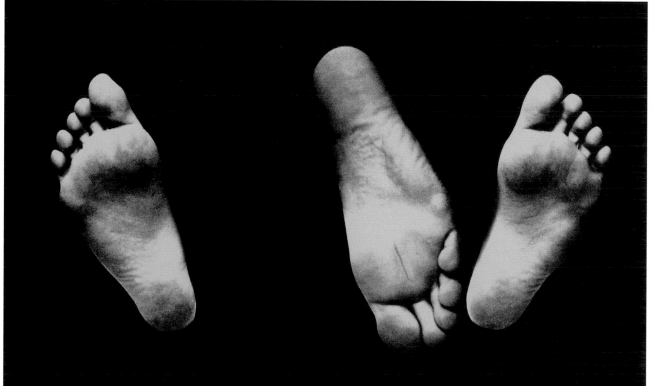

SARAJEVO HUMOR

Title: **Sarajevo Postcard Collection**
Format: **Postcards**
Art Director/Designers: **Trio Sarajevo**
Client: **No client**
Country: **Bosnia and Herzegovina**
Year: **1993**

To convey the idea of suffering in Sarajevo, artists used any available images including pop and visual icons.

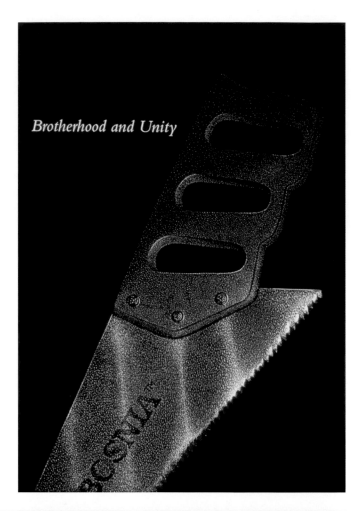

Title: **Brotherhood
and Unity**
Format: **Poster**
Art Director/Designer:
Cedomir Kostović
Client: **Southwest
Missouri State University**
Country: **USA**
Year: **1994**

The three-holed handle of
this bloody saw signifies
the three ethnic and
religious groups (Serbs,
Croats, and Muslims)
contributing to the
destruction and devastation
of Bosnia. "Brotherhood
and Unity" was a
communist slogan used to
keep the groups united.
This poster suggests that
what they are actually
working together to
accomplish is the
destruction of Bosnia.

Title: **Bosnia
(Sea of Blood)**
Format: **Poster**
Art Director/Designer:
Cedomir Kostović
Client: **Southwest
Missouri State University**
Country: **USA**
Year: **1994**

This strong and effective
use of typography suggests
that at the time this poster
was designed, Bosnia was
drowning in a sea of blood.

Title: **Bosnia (Divided)**
Format: **Poster**
Art Director/Designer:
Cedomir Kostović
Client: **Southwest Missouri State University**
Country: **USA**
Year: **1994**

The division of Bosnia is represented by this violin, now in three pieces, which has been dismantled and made into a useless object, no longer capable of creating music. For Bosnia/the violin to work again, the country's three religious groups (Serbs, Croats, and Muslims) must reunite and work together.

BOSNIA

Title: **Glazbeni Dozivljaji**
Format: **Poster**
Art Director/Designer/
Illustrator: **Boris Bućan**
Client: **Zagrebački
Simfoničari I Zbor HRTV**
Country: **Croatia**
Year: **1990–91**

This series of posters was
created for the Zagreb
Philharmonic Orchestra
just prior to, and during
the beginning of, the
Serbo/Croatian war. The
illustrations subtly depict a
war within an orchestra by
showing musicians fighting
against each other.

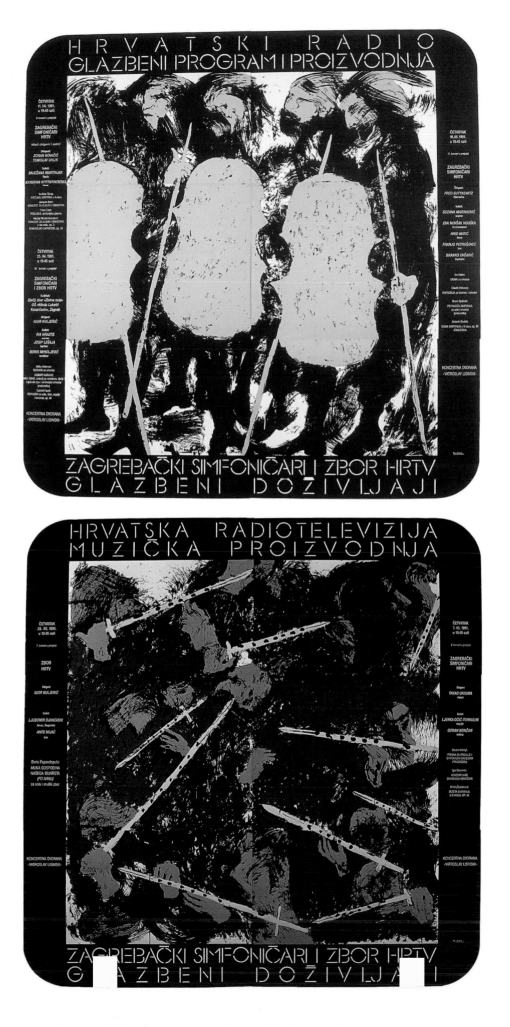

Title: **Dubrovnik**
Format: **Poster**
Art Director/Designer:
Illustrator: **Boris Bućan**
Client: **Unknown**
Country: **Croatia**
Year: **1992**

The St. Laurence Fortress
has become the symbol of
Dubrovnik within the
tourism industry. On this
poster, however, which was
created during the Croatian
war for independence and
the siege of Dubrovnik, it
became a symbolic
defender of the city.

Title: **War**
Format: **Folder**
Art Director/Designer:
Mirko Ilić
Client: **Tony Mandić**
Country: **USA**
Year: **1991**

This folder was designed to hold information about a Los Angeles fund-raising event to support victims of the war in Croatia. *(top)*

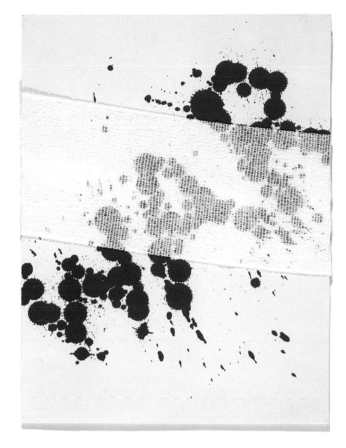

Title: **SOS Croatia**
Format: **Poster**
Art Director/Designer:
Ranko Novak
Client: **Art Directors Club Ljubljana**
Country: **Slovenia**
Year: **1991**

This poster uses a red checkerboard, the symbol of Croatia since medieval times, shown bleeding and splattered with blood as an SOS (Morse code distress signal) against the aggression in Croatia. *(bottom left)*

Title: **Krvatska!**
Format: **Poster and T-shirts**
Art Director/Designer:
Boris Ljubicić
Client: **HO2**
Country: **Croatia**
Year: **Unknown**

This plea to the world to pay attention to Croatia cleverly switches letters in "Hrvatska," the Croatian spelling of Croatia, to get its point across. By changing the H to a K, the Croat word for blood— "krv"—is formed. *(bottom right)*

Title: **Read Between the Lines**
Format: **Poster**
Art Director/Designer: **Boris Ljubicić**
Client: **No client**
Country: **Croatia**
Year: **1994**

The text on this poster, designed to be read from a short distance, was written by the survivors of the massacre of Vukovar, sometimes known as the Croatian Stalingrad because of its total destruction. The piece commemorating the third anniversary of the occupation of Vukovar, in which 700 of its defenders and 1,600 civilians were killed, and 2,600 of its inhabitants disappeared without a trace, asks for the liberation and return of its people.

Title: **Serbian Cutting**
Format: **Magazine**
Art Director/Designers: **Dejan Krsić, Dejan Dragosavac Rutta**
Client: *Bastard* magazine
Country: **Slovenia and Serbia**
Year: **1998**

New Moment (visual communications, design, and arts magazine) offered the designers space to promote their magazine for free, so the designers wanted to use that opportunity to raise awareness about crimes of official Serbian politics on Kosovo. They cleverly chose a headline that refers to avant-garde film montage in Serbian cinema as well as images of the atrocities being committed against Albanian citizens in Kosovo. Subsequently, the design was rejected by *New Moment*, but was later published in the first issue of *Bastard* magazine.

Title: **Mi smo se borili
da bi se vi danas borili**
Format: **Poster**
Art Director/Designers:
Albino Ursić, Boris Kuk
Client: **No client**
Country: **Croatia**
Year: **1993**

This photograph of World
War II partisan fighters,
combined with the
message, "we fought (for
unity) so you can fight (to
break apart) now," is a
sarcastic jab at the
struggle between various groups in
Croatia. The text at the top
of the poster reads "Party
of recovered partisans."

Title: **Fascist Groove**
Format: **Poster
and postcard**
Art Director/Designer:
Dejan Krsić
Client: **Self, NGO
"Moj Glas"**
Country: **Croatia**
Year: **2002**

Posters and postcards take
the theme from the song of
a German rock band named
Heaven 17: "We don't need
this fascist groove thing."
The cover text accuses the
political party HDZ of
promoting intolerance.
The postcard, featuring the
Prime Minister holding his
right hand in the air, comes
preprinted with the address
of the Croatian parliament
on the back (right) so the
reader can easily send it.
This work was done during
the Croatian general's trial
at the Hague International
Court for War Crimes.

kosovo
risiko

Gioko di guerra

Title: **Kosovo Risiko**
Format: **Poster**
Art Director/Designer:
Andrea Rauch
Client: **No client**
Country: **Italy**
Year: **1999**

Created in opposition to
the war in Kosovo, this
poster uses a play on words
between Kosovo and Risiko,
a popular Italian "gioko di
guerra," or war game.

L'impossible

Dragoljub Zamurović, Oslobađanje Vukovara, 1991. (GAMMA PRESS IMAGE; PARIS MATCH)

Title: **L'impossible**
Format: **Flyer**
Art Director/Designer:
Stanislav Sharp
Client: **Art Group FIA**
Country: **Serbia
and Montenegro**
Year: **1993**

This flyer, which was
distributed in Serbia,
featured an image of
Serbian soldiers riding
through the ruined, a.k.a.
"liberated," streets of
Vukovar, proving that
soldiers from Serbia took
part in the war in Croatia,
a fact that was not
acknowledged by the
Serbian media.

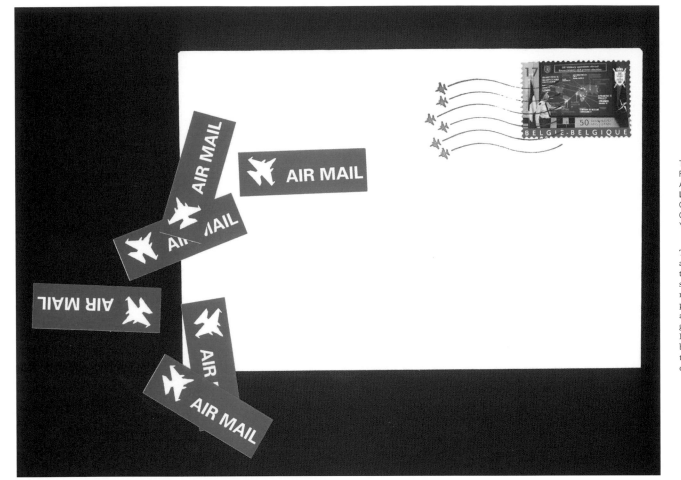

Title: **Airmail**
Format: **Airmail sticker**
Art Director/Designers:
Lisa Boxus and Skart
Client: **No client**
Country: **Belgium**
Year: **1999**

The simple substitution of a fighter plane effectively transforms the airmail sticker into a warning that no one can stay out of politics. FRONT is an art activism against violence group, which is based in Brussels and was initiated by Skart who distributed these as an act of civil disobedience.

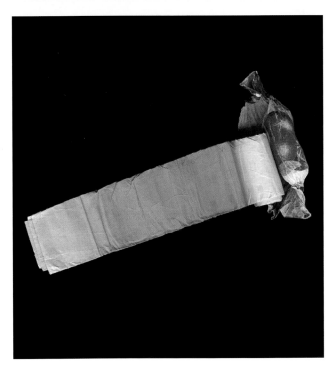

BANG!

(YOU ARE DEAD)

FRONT

Title: **Bombon**
Format: **Candy wrapper**
Art Director/Designers:
**Philippe Hulet
and Skart**
Client: **No client**
Country: **Belgium**
Year: **1999**

The desirability of imported Belgium bonbons is lost upon the opening of a "Bombon," which appears to be a wrapped candy, but is actually a rolled piece of paper revealing the sad reality of NATO participating in war instead of providing humanitarian aid. The Bombons were distributed during the NATO aggression of Yugoslavia in 1999.

Title: **Postcards
to Milošević**
Format: **Postcards**
Art Director/Designer:
Nikola Kostandinović
Client:
Organization Otpor
Country: **Serbia
and Montenegro**
Year: **2000**

Organization Otpor is
an independent,
nongovernmental
organization whose
activists played a crucial
role in the street
demonstrations that began
immediately following
the elections and led to
Slobodan Milošević's
downfall. "Otpor" in
Serbian means "resistance,"
and the organization was
founded in the mid-1990s
by students from Belgrade
University and elsewhere
in Serbia, who had had
enough of Milošević's
chokehold on the neck
of the Serbian society.
Between 1999 and 2001,
more than 1,500 Otpor
activists (of about 50,000
based in more than ten
Serbian cities) were arrested
and interrogated by security
forces under Milošević's
control. This series of postcards mocking Milošović
was pre-addressed to be
sent to Milošević's home.

Gospodine Miloševiću,
Posle deset godina
nesreće koju ste Vi doneli
bivšoj Jugoslaviji,
Srbiji i srpskom narodu,
vreme je da se povučete
dok ne bude kasno za
Vas i za nas.

UPUTSTVO:
Ukoliko se slažete sa ovom porukom
samo zalepite poštansku marku,
potpišite se i ovu razglednicu ubacite
u prvo poštansko sanduče.

G-din Slobodan
Milošević
11000 Beograd
Užička 16
Srbija

Title: **Got Oil?**
Format: **Poster**
Art Director/Designers:
Nenad Cizl, Toni Tomašek
Client: **Magdalena Young
Creatives Festival**
Country: **Slovenia**
Year: **2004**

Part of the power of this
poster depends on the
viewer's knowledge of the
"Got Milk?" ad campaign
for the American Dairy
Association in which the
subjects featured are
always shown with a "milk
mustache." In this parody,
Bush's lips are smeared
with oil creating a
vampirelike image, alluding
to his passion for oil.

Title: **Blind**
Format: **Digital postcards**
Art Director/Designers
**Sonia Freeman,
Gabriel Freeman**
Client: **Un Mundo Feliz/A
Happy World Production**
Country: **Spain**
Year: **2003**

These posters were created
for an exhibition in
Portland, Oregon entitled:
"The Language of Terror:
anti-war.us graphics" in
which all works were
wildposted to a single wall.
The first two images create
a parallel between Bush's
and Saddam's blindness in
the war, and the final image
reflects how we were all
affected by their blindness.

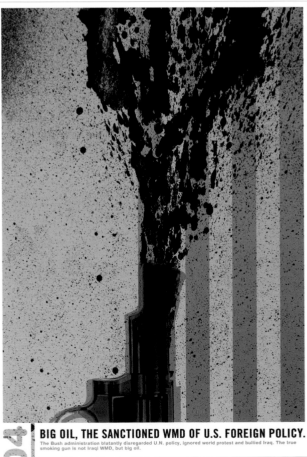

BIG OIL, EXPLOITING U.S. FOREIGN POLICY SINCE 2001.
Prior to becoming president, George W. Bush honed his executive skills by driving three oil exploration corporations to financial ruin. Now, he's determined to do the same to America.

BIG OIL, LUBRICATING U.S. FOREIGN POLICY SINCE 2001.
Former Halliburton CEO and current U.S. vice president, Dick Cheney, still receives deferred salary from Halliburton—the world's largest oil field services corporation.

BIG OIL, FUELING U.S. FOREIGN POLICY SINCE 2001.
Former director of Chevron, Condoleezza Rice accepted the highest honor Chevron could bestow— a supertanker named Condoleezza Rice.

BIG OIL, THE SANCTIONED WMD OF U.S. FOREIGN POLICY.
The Bush administration blatantly disregarded U.N. policy, ignored world protest and bullied Iraq. The true smoking gun is not Iraqi WMD, but big oil.

Title: **Big Oil**
Format: **Poster series**
Art Director/Designer:
May L. Sorum
Client: **No client**
Country: **USA**
Year: **2004**

The Big Oil poster series uses oil-splattered portraits of George Bush, Dick Cheney, and Condoleezza Rice to draw parallels between the oil interests of the Bush Administration and American political policy. At the bottom of each poster, direct connections between the people featured and the oil industry are simply stated.

Title: **Death Flag
(America, Where
Have You Gone?)**
Format: **Poster**
Art Director/Designer:
Adrienne Burk
Client: **No client**
Country: **USA**
Year: **2003**

In this bold and simple
image, the designer creates
an American flag out of
blood and oil, suggesting
America has forgotten
constitutional ideals. The
poster was used at anti-Iraq
war protests.

America, where have you gone?

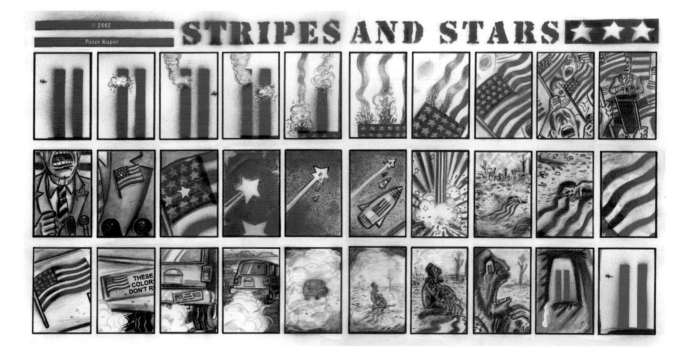

Title: **Stripes and Stars**
Format: **Comic**
Art Director/Designer:
Carrie Whitney
Illustrator: **Peter Kuper**
Client:
The Comics Journal
Country: **USA**
Year: **2002**

This comic strip was
created for the special
patriotism issue of *The
Comics Journal*, a vigorous
antagonist of the Bush
Administration, suggesting
how an endless war on
terrorism would create an
endless cycle of violence.

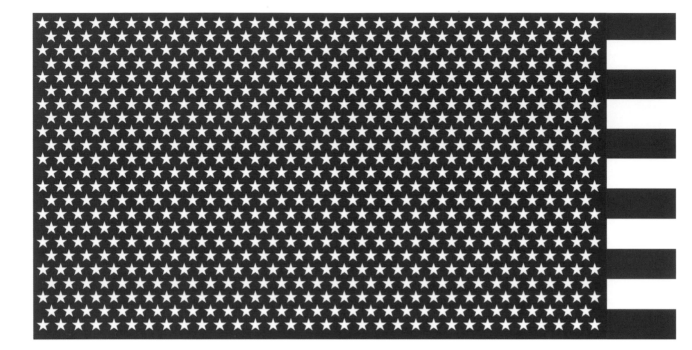

Title: **American Flag**
Format: **Poster**
Art Director/Designers:
Nenad Cizl, Toni Tomašek
Client: *Mladina* magazine
Country: **Slovenia**
Year: **2003**

In this poster commenting on American politics around the globe, the American flag shown has grown from 50 stars, each representing a state within the United States, to an innumerable number.

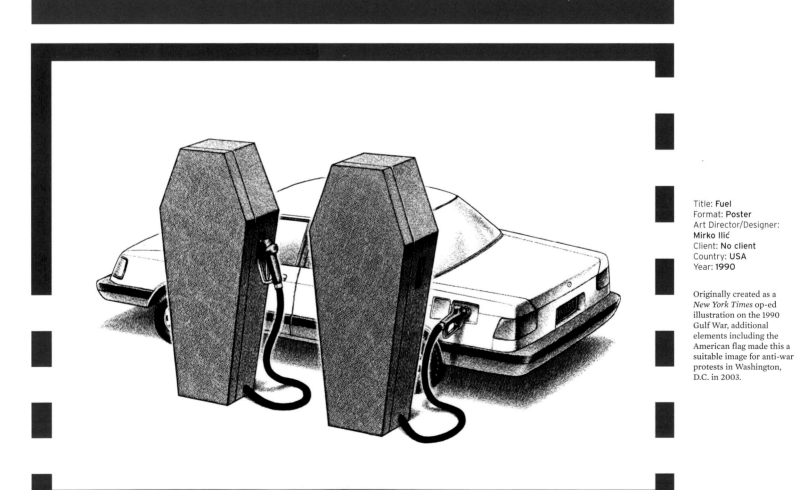

Title: **Fuel**
Format: **Poster**
Art Director/Designer:
Mirko Ilić
Client: **No client**
Country: **USA**
Year: **1990**

Originally created as a *New York Times* op-ed illustration on the 1990 Gulf War, additional elements including the American flag made this a suitable image for anti-war protests in Washington, D.C. in 2003.

Title: **Guided Missiles**
Format: **Postcard**
Art Director/Designer:
Joe Miller
Client:
AnotherPosterForPeace.org
Country: **USA**
Year: **2003**

The powerful quote by
Martin Luther King, Jr.
comparing "guided
missiles" to "misguided
men" is paralleled by a
strong image of missiles
imposed on the Earth.
This bold imagery indicates
that our technology of
destruction has redefined
the way conflicts are
resolved and that "humanity
and weaponry are set at
odds."

our scientific power has outrun our spiritual power. we have guided missiles and misguided men. *martin luther king, jr.*

USA en IRAK ¡No a la guerra!

Title: **USA in Irak. Not
to War**
Format: **Poster**
Art Director/Designer:
Renato Aranda Rodríguez
Client: **No client**
Country: **Mexico**
Year: **2003**

By transforming a map of
the United States into a
meat cleaver, the designer
makes a powerful comment
on the U.S. bombing of Iraq.
The first information
received in Mexico at the
beginning of the war was
that the attacks were
"surgical," a reference
to the precision of the
missiles. This work speaks
to the arrogance of the
term, as "there is no war
where only the bad people
die."

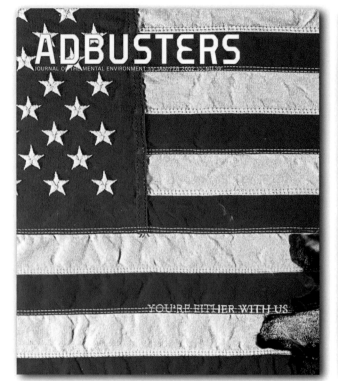

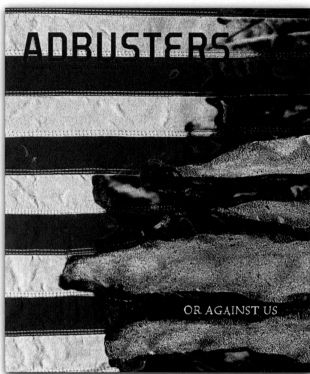

Title: *Adbusters*
Issue #39
Format: **Magazine cover**
Art Director/Designer:
**Adbusters
Media Foundation**
Photographer:
Randall Cosco
Client: *Adbusters*
Country: **Canada**
Year: **2002**

This issue was the first published after September 11, 2001. The gravity of the event caused the magazine to shift its focus slightly, with subsequent issues placing more emphasis on U.S. foreign policy. *(top)*

Title: Will Kill for Oil
Format: **T-shirt**
Client: **No client**
Art Director/Designer:
Christopher Loch
Country: **USA**
Year: **2004**

A satirical design based on the phrase "Will work for food" has been used for T-shirts, postcards, and stickers. The posture of a begging Bush reminds everyone that the continuing cooperation of Americans is needed to sustain his policies. *(bottom left)*

Title: Oil Habit
Format: **T-shirt**
Art Director/Designers:
**Scott Palmer,
Keeno Ahmed**
Client: **No client**
Country: **USA**
Year: **2004**

This skull comprising 1,000 oil rigs, comments on the global dependency for oil and its disastrous effects politically and environmentally. *(bottom right)*

Title: **First Killing/Oil Spill**
Format: **Leaflets**
Art Director/Designer:
Dennis Edge
Client: **No client**
Country: **USA**
Year: **2004**

These two images were part of a series of leaflets alerting people about the dangerous consequences of irresponsible oil consumption. *(top)*

Title: **War on Terror**
Format: **Poster**
Art Director/Designers:
**Marty Neumeier,
Josh Levine**
Client:
AnotherPosterForPeace.org
Country: **USA**
Year: **2004**

In response to the events of September 11, this poster aptly suggests "applying technological violence to terrorism is like pouring gas on a fire...the viewer knows exactly what to expect if the gas is poured." *(top right)*

Title: **anti-war.us**
Format: **Website**
Art Director/Curator:
Joshua Berger
Designer: **Jon Steinhorst**
Interface designer:
Anthony Ramos
Client: **No client**
Country: **USA**
Year: **2002**

The anti-war.us website was created by Plazm Design to distribute effective anti-war messages and graphics to activists around the world. The intention is to make the images available to the public for downloading so that they can be transferred to stickers, posters, signs, or other media for posting. *(bottom)*

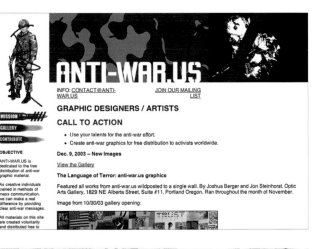

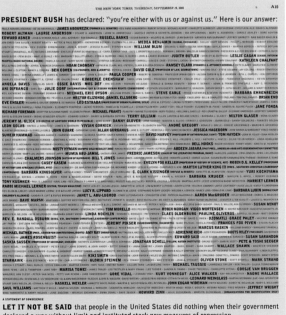

Title: War on Iraq?
Format: Billboard
Art Director/Designer:
Noah Scalin
Client: Richmond
Peace Coalition
Country: USA
Year: 2003

"Not in our name" became a phrase used by the peace movement before the war in Iraq was initiated. The campaign was originally planned as a series of billboards with a variety of messages but reverted to a single location after the original billboard company refused to run the series due to its content. *(top)*

Title: Not In Our Name
Format: Newspaper ad
Art Director/Designers:
Sheila Levrant de Bretteville, Scott Stowell, Susan Barber
Client: Not In Our Name
Country: USA
Year: 2002

Not In Our Name is a coalition of Americans dedicated to peace and civil liberties for all. This full-page newspaper ad features the Not In Our Name Statement of Conscience and the names of some of the thousands of people who support this open letter to George Bush/ad which was published in the *New York Times* on September 19, 2002. *(bottom left)*

Title: Don't Buy It.
Format: Poster
Art Director/Designer:
Kimberly Cross
Client:
AnotherPosterForPeace.org
Country: USA
Year: 2003

By asking viewers to boycott the war, the artist is commenting on the notion that the war was sold to the American public as if it were a product. *(bottom right)*

Title: *The Nation*
Initiative Buttons
Format: Buttons
Art Director/Designer:
Milton Glaser
Client: *The Nation*
magazine
Country: USA
Year: 2003-2004

This series of pre-Iraq war
buttons were sold by the
The Nation to its readers
and were widely circulated.

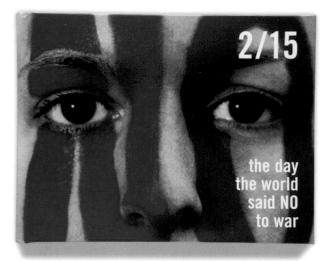

Title: *2/15: The Day
the World Said No to War*
Format: **Book**
Art Director/Designer:
Connie Koch
Client: **Hello [NYC],
All Press**
Country: **USA**
Year: **2003**

Thirty million people in
thirty-eight countries gathered to protest the immi-
nent U.S. invasion of Iraq
on February 15, 2003. The
photographs and comments
were collected via email
and used to produce the
book *2/15*. The designers
hope this reminder of the
pressure that civil power
can exert on governments
will inspire continued
involvement.

London

We've never really seen a movement like this before — it's unpredictable because it's so unprecedented. But it does seem that a large proportion of the people who participated [on February 15th] are becoming quite politicized just by going to the demonstration.

PAUL ROGERS PROFESSOR OF PEACE STUDIES AT BRADFORD UNIVERSITY

LONDON
ENGLAND
2.15.03
PHOTO BY
JESS HURD
REPORT DIGITAL

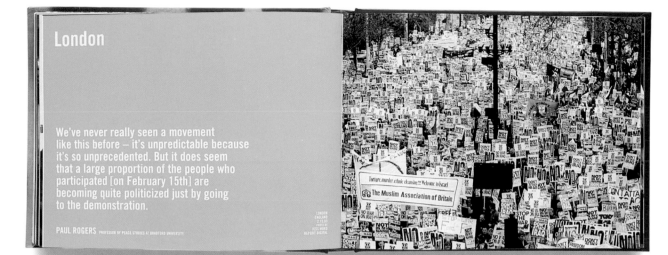

BYRON BAY
AUSTRALIA
2.2.03
PHOTO BY
PETER & LISA CARRETTE
ICON IMAGES PTY LTD
NUDE NO WAR PROTEST

Finally, the World is united! (against us)

WASHINGTON D.C.
USA
3.15.03
PHOTO BY
SONDA DAWES
THE IMAGE WORKS

211

Our Nation's cause has always been larger than our Nation's defense. We fight, as we always fight, for a just peace — a peace that favors liberty. We will defend the peace against the threats from terrorists and tyrants. We will preserve the peace by building good relations among the great powers. And we will extend the peace by encouraging free and open societies on every continent.

GEORGE W. BUSH
PRESIDENT OF THE UNITED STATES OF AMERICA ON THE NATIONAL SECURITY STRATEGY OF THE UNITED STATES, 6.1.2002

Title: *NOZONE IX EMPIRE*
Format: **Comic book**
Art Director/Designers:
**Nicholas Blechman,
Naomi Mizusaki,
Stefan Sagmeister**
Client: **Princeton
University Press**
Country: **USA**
Year: **2004**

NOZONE, a political satirical comic book, rises far
above the *MAD* magazine
genre. The variety and skill
of its contributors such as
Johnny Sweetwater's "The
Eagle Has Landed" *(top)*
and Stefan Sagmeister with
"I Am Not An Imperialist"
(bottom) in this issue on
"Empire," creates crackling
visual textures and
literary vitality.

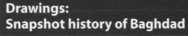

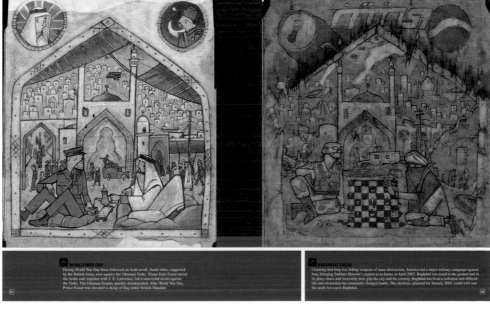

Title: *Diplo* magazine
Format: **Magazine**
Art Director/Designer:
Diplo magazine
Client: *Diplo* magazine
Country: United Kingdom
Year: 2004

The December 2004
edition of *Diplo*, a monthly
international affairs
magazine, examined
whether the West is at war
with Islam. The cover
features mirrored images of
George Bush and Osama
bin Laden, representing
their mutual clash of
fundamentalism. The
magazine featured Bush on
the cover with English text
and bin Laden on the back
with the same text in
Arabic, allowing the
magazine to be sold in both
the Western and Arab
worlds. The goal of the
magazine was to show an
accessible but definitive
history of Baghdad,
through a series of illustrations about a city at the
heart of the Islamic world.

Title: **Taking Liberties**
Format: **Magazine cover**
Art Director/Designer:
Peter Kuper
Illustrator: **Mirko Ilić**
Client: *World War 3*
Country: **USA**
Year: **2004**

Originally published in
the *Village Voice*, this
illustration was later reused
by *World War 3*—one of
the longest operating
alternative magazines in
the United States—for a
special issue dedicated to
the war in Iraq.

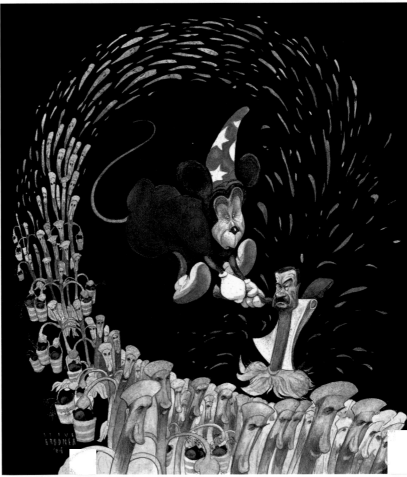

Title: **Fantasia**
Format: **Watercolor
on paper**
Illustrator: **Steve Brodner**
Client: **No client**
Country: **USA**
Year: **2004**

A Disney image from
Fantasia is used as a
metaphor for George W.
Bush's contempt for
Saddam Hussein. Bush is
seen here smashing
Hussein, creating hundreds
of Osama bin Ladens in the
process. This unsolicited
illustration was offered to
and rejected by *New Yorker,
Mother Jones,* and *The
Nation.*

Title: **Iraq War Posters**
Format: **Poster series**
Art Director/Designers:
Kevin Wade, Jim Lasser
Client: **No client**
Country: **USA**
Year: **2003-2004**

The true strength in these contradictory posters, which feature catchy copy that could easily accompany a joyful seasonal advertisement, is their element of surprise and simplicity.

iRaq

10,000 volts in your pocket, guilty or innocent.

Title: **iRaq**
Format: **Poster**
Art Director/Designer:
Copper Greene
Client: **No client**
Country: **USA**
Year: **2004**

This parody of an
advertising campaign for
iPod uses a horrifying
image of torture from the
military prison in Abu
Ghraib to protest the U.S.
occupation of Iraq. The
designer posted these
confrontational posters
among the iPod posters
(below), resulting in a
surprising and powerful
effect.

Title: **Non-Suicide
Bomber**
Format: **Postcard**
Art Director/Designer:
Chaz Maviyane-Davies
Client: **No client**
Country: **USA**
Year: **2004**

This piece was inspired by
a radio interview the
designer heard in which an
Iraqi ironically referred to
the actions of the United
States as "non-suicide
bombers."

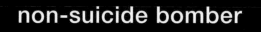

non-suicide bomber

Title: **Victory?**
Format: **Poster**
Art Director/Designer:
Jadran Boban
Client: **Syracuse
Anti-War Demo**
Country: **Croatia**
Year: **2003**

An ironic victory is shown
by using the most popular
symbol of the Second
World War to create the
message that every war
victory leaves death behind.
The work, created for
anti-war demonstrations in
Syracuse, New York, was
distributed over the
Internet and taped up
around the city as a call to
and promotion for
demonstrations.

Title: **Alternative Street Sign**
Format: **Poster series**
Art Director/Designer: **Michael Duffy**
Client: **No client**
Country: **USA**
Year: **2003**

This series of stenciled signs was surreptitiously affixed to traffic poles by volunteers working at off-peak hours to "agitate driver peripheral perception and contribute to general road anxiety." The work was a "reaction to America's blissful ignorance to the dark future of Bush's nightmares."

Mom, We're Home!

Title: **Mom, We're Home!**
Format: **Poster**
Art Director/Designer:
John Yates
Client: **Stealworks**
Country: **USA**
Year: **1987**

This generic anti-war piece was used during the first Gulf War. It was later used by the Center for the Study of Political Graphics' art show "The Price of Intervention" in Los Angeles in 1991. A decade and a half later, the work feels equally poignant in regard to the fact that during the second Gulf War, the U.S. government censored photos of the returning dead, justifying this censorship as a matter of respect for the victims.

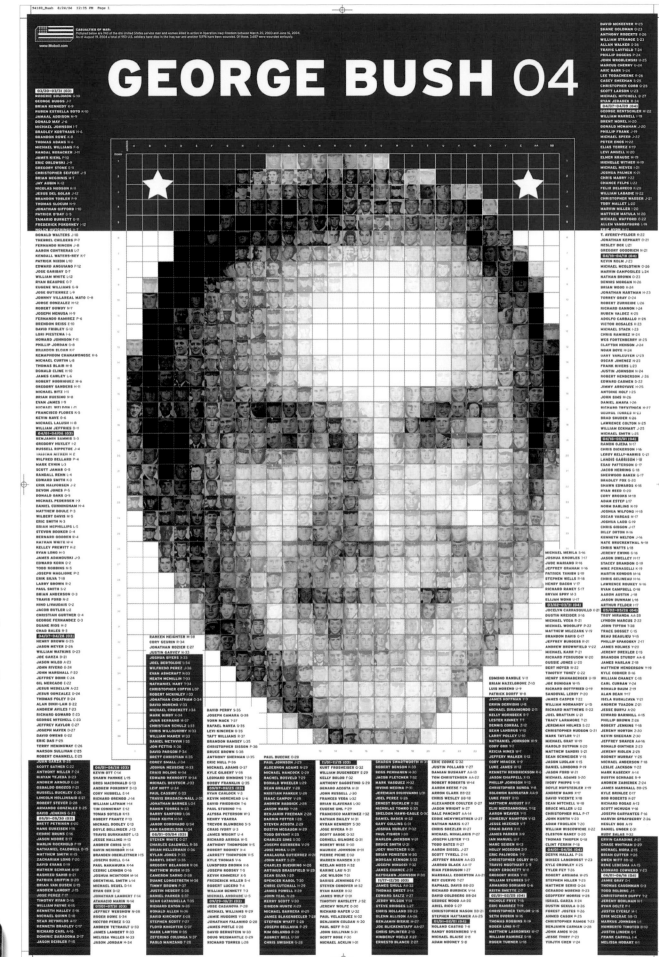

Title: Casualties of War
Format: Poster
Art Director/Designer:
Daniel Jasper
Client: No client
Country: USA
Year: 2004

Tired of simplistic frothing at the mouth anti-Bush messages? This artist constructed his poster to withstand changes in both the environmental and political points of view. Using computer technology, the faces of individual soldiers who have lost their lives up to that point in the Iraq war have been used to construct George Bush's face, while the names of all the soldiers are listed around his image. In addition to the poster, the designer had tie tacks made of the flag draped coffin illustration (top left corner) as seen below.

Title: **Peace**
Format: **Poster**
Art Director/Designer:
Stanley Eisenman
Client: **Moratorium
Committee**
Country: **USA**
Year: **1970**

In this poster, the American
flag represents the P in the
word "peace" and conveys
in a simple and powerful
way that the United States
should get out of Vietnam.

Title: War—What Is
It Good For?
Format: **Poster**
Art Director/Designer:
Marty Neumeier
Client:
AnotherPosterForPeace.org
Country: **USA**
Year: **2004**

Contrasting a raw,
emotional typeface with a
measured, thoughtful one,
this artist captures the
conflict between passion
and reason, war and peace.
The message is from the
first line of a song, popular
in the early 1970s.

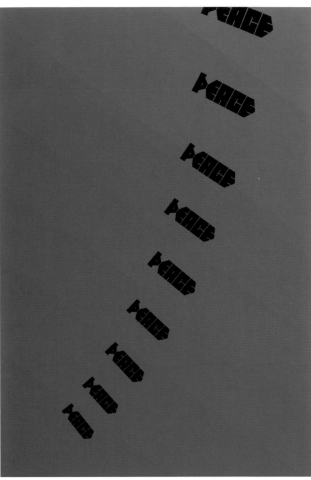

Title: **Your Name Here**
Format: **Poster**
Art Director/Designer:
Ellen Gould
Client:
AnotherPosterForPeace.org
Country: **USA**
Year: **2003**

Writing personal messages
on bombs became a
common practice during
WWII. Here that space is
offered for corporate
advertising in this free,
downloadable poster
available on the Internet.
(top left)

Title: **Bombing Peace**
Format: **Poster**
Art Director/Designer:
Samuli Viitasaari
Client: **No client**
Country: **Finland**
Year: **2003**

This poster, posted in and
around Kuopio, Finland,
contemplates how easily
people adapt to and believe
even the "harshest lies," as
long as they are told to us
by our leaders. The designer
notes that it's almost as if
there is a switch that can be
flicked to turn off an entire
nation's common sense,
whereby aggression is
suddenly seen as a sign of
good-heartedness, while
attempts to avoid violence
make one a no-good traitor.
(top right)

Title: **NO War**
Format: **New Year's
greetings card**
Art Director/Designer:
Patrick Thomas
Client: **Studio la Vista**
Country: **Spain**
Year: **2002**

A 2003 New Year's greeting
card in the form of a stencil
gave recipients the tool to
actively oppose the
impending war in Iraq.
(middle & bottom)

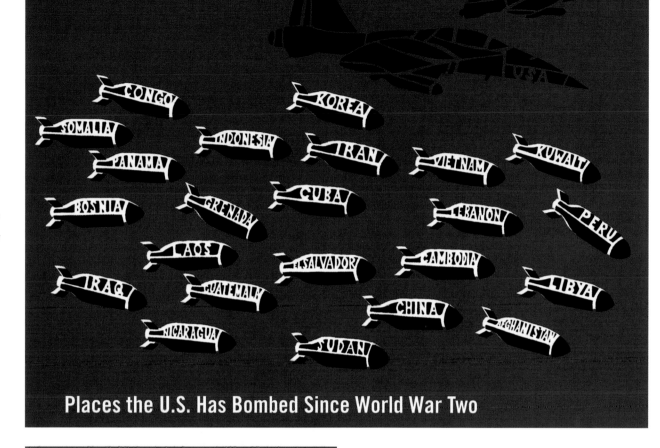

Title: **Places the U.S. Has Bombed Since World War Two**
Format: **Poster**
Art Director/Designer: **Josh MacPhee**
Client: **No client**
Country: **USA**
Year: **2002**

Falling bombs with the names of the countries the United States has bombed since World War II convey the scope and shocking impact of U.S. foreign policy since WWII.

Places the U.S. Has Bombed Since World War Two

Title: **Endgame**
Format: **Poster**
Art Director/Designer: **Milton Glaser**
Client: **Lawyer's Committee on Nuclear Policy**
Country: **USA**
Year: **2004**

The word endgame was intended to have two meanings. The first refers to the fact that ignoring nuclear proliferation could lead to the end of life on earth. The second reflects the idea that it is time to end that threat altogether.

ENDGAME

IT'S 2005, TIME TO END THE THREAT OF NUCLEAR ANNIHILATION. JOIN THE YEAR OF REMEMBRANCE AND ACTION FOR A NUCLEAR WEAPON FREE WORLD.

Title: We Don't Need
Another Hiro
Format: **Poster**
Art Director/Designer:
Yossi Lemel
Client: **No client**
Country: **Israel**
Year: **2003**

This poster, which
coincides with the fiftieth
anniversary of the bombing
of Hiroshima, is an
expression of protest
against France's decision to
renew its nuclear testing on
the Mururoa islands.
Changing "Hero" to "Hiro"
in this well-known musical
lyric serves as a historical
reminder of how easily
good intentions can lead to
tragedy.

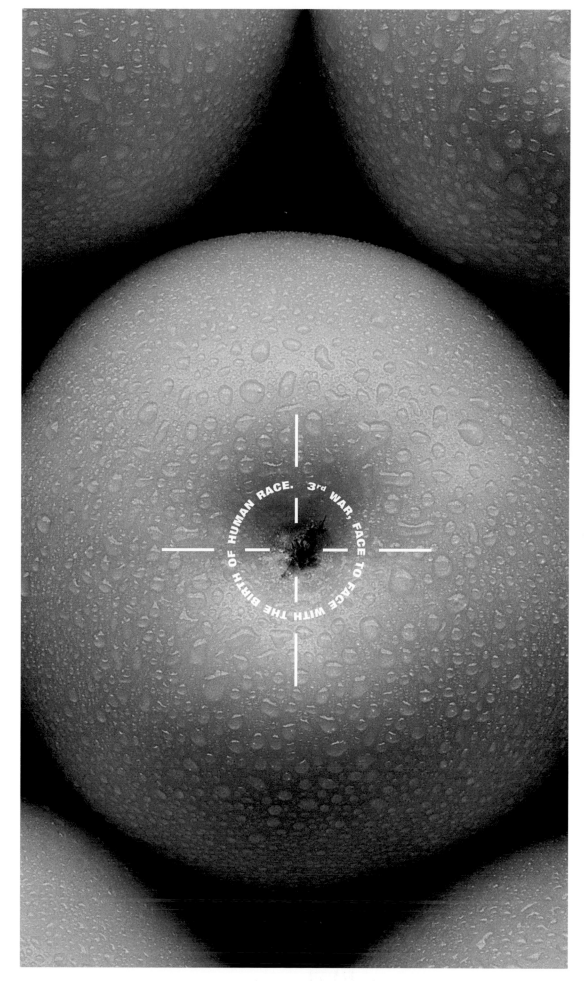

Title: **Third War**
Format: **Poster**
Art Director/Designer:
Tahamtan Aminian
Client: **Fioreh Publication**
Country: **Iran**
Year: **2003**

The apples in this picture
cleverly suggest a pregnant
woman targeted by the
possibility of a third world
war and, as a result, the
extinction of the human
race.

Title: **POW For Peace**
Format: **Magazine cover**
Art Director/Designers:
Mike Salisbury, Lloyd Ziff
Client: *Rolling Stone*
Country: **USA**
Year: **1973**

This cover for *Rolling Stone*, produced during the Vietnam War, illustrates the realities soldiers faced when they chose not to fight and were, as a result, confronted by their own comrades.

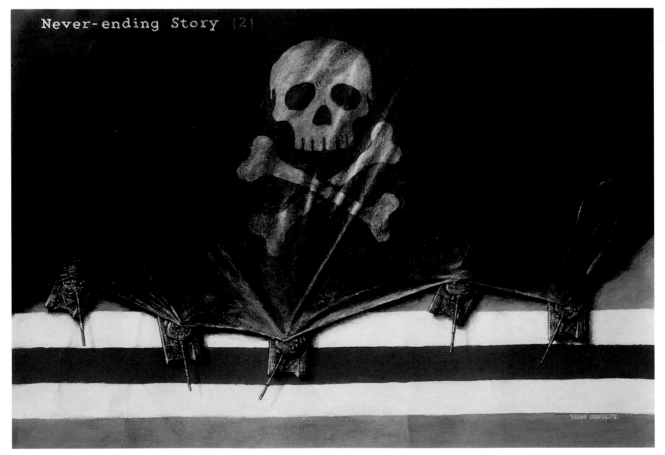

Title: **Never-ending Story**
Format: **Poster**
Art Director/Designer:
Wieslaw Grzegorczyk
Client: **No client**
Country: **Poland**
Year: **2002**

Tanks are seen here pulling the Jolly Roger flag over the Chechnyan flag symbolizing the return of the Russian army in Chechnya. The Jolly Roger is the flag flown by pirates, many armies, and paramilitary groups and is a universal symbol of death.

Title: **Don't Bush Putin**
Format: **T-Shirt**
Art Director/Designers:
Jaka Modić, Bojan Senjur
Client: **Dajmo Stisnt Teater**
Country: **Slovenia**
Year: **2001**

A Slovenian theater group
wore these T-shirts while
performing as part of a
peaceful protest during the
George Bush–Vladimir
Putin summit in 2001. One
of the most closely watched
parts of the discussions was
strategic arms control.

Title: **Alternatives to War**
Format: **Poster**
Art Director/Designers:
**Joe Scorsone,
Alice Drueding**
Client: **SDPosters.com**
Country: **USA**
Year: **2003**

Military figures are shown
taking part in peaceful
pursuits to remind those
with the power not to send
troops to war because we
have only one chance to
experience the joys of
everyday life. This poster
is part of a series that was
started in 1995 for
promotional purposes.

Title: **WAR = DEATH**
Format: **Poster**
Art Director/Designer:
Michael Mabry
Client:
AnotherPosterForPeace.org
Country: **USA**
Year: **2003**

This copyright-free poster
was specifically designed
for free downloads.
Another Poster for Peace
is an organization created
in response to the Bush
Administration's brilliant
pro-war marketing.
Design is used to support
a grassroots anti-campaign:
"If enough of us voice our
dissent, we will be heard."
(top left)

Title: **WAR—I hate
this game**
Format: **Antiwar sign**
Art Director/Designer:
Jugoslav Vlahović
Client: *NIN* **weekly
newspaper**
Country: **Serbia and
Montenegro**
Year: **1999**

The NBA logo, which is
well-known in Serbia and
Montenegro because of
their successful team, was
appropriated to make this
antiwar sign. The newly
created logo was very
popular in Yugoslavia,
appearing on T-shirts, in
magazines, and over the
Internet during the NATO
bombings in 1999.
(top right)

Title: **Pentagon:
Bloody Red**
Format: **Poster**
Art Director/Designer:
**Alireza Mostafazadeh
Ebrahimi**
Client: **Negar**
Country: **Iran**
Year: **2004**

The creator of this poster
uses a Pantone color chip,
the most commonly used
color matching system
by design professionals, as
a way of representing
America's war policies, and
suggesting that "Bloody
Red" may be the only color
the Pentagon knows.
(bottom)

MAKE UP, NOT WAR

Thea Line cosmetics

Title: **Make Up, Not War**
Format: **Cosmetics ad**
Art Director/Designer:
Igor Avzner
Client: **Thea Line
cosmetics**
Country: **Serbia and
Montenegro**
Year: **Unknown**

This antiwar advertisement,
produced by a cosmetics
company in Serbia, replaced
bullets in a cartridge belt
with lipstick. It was used by
militia to convey its hope
for peace.

Title: **Burnt**
Format: **Holiday card**
Art Director/Designer:
Lisa Gibson
Client: **No client**
Country: **USA**
Year: **2003**

During a season of warm
wishes and good cheer, it is
especially poignant to
receive a holiday card
focused on how peace, the
most vital thread keeping
our world united and
healthy, has been burned
and broken.

better luck
next year
Peace on Earth

Title: **The Iran for
Land Peace**
Format: **Poster**
Art Director/Designer:
Mehdi Saeedi
Client: **Sepah**
Country: **Iran**
Year: **Unknown**

The words Iran Land
of Peace are repeated in
different sizes to construct
a nest for this fragile bird.

Title: **Peace**
Format: **Electronic poster**
Art Director/Designer:
**Mr. Tharp
(inspired by Sam Smidt)**
Client:
AnotherPosterForPeace.org
Country: **USA**
Year: **2003**

This downloadable
electronic image was
designed for
AnotherPosterForPeace.org,
an online source for
copyright-free images
promoting peace.

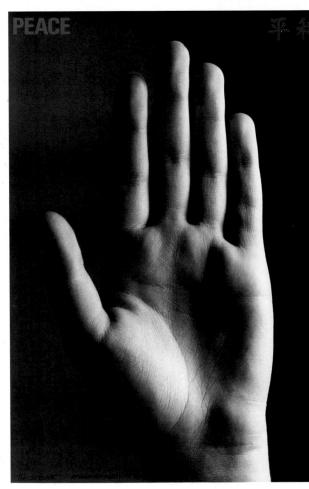

Title: **King Kong & Godzilla**
Format: **Poster**
Art Director/Designer: **Steff Geissbuhler**
Client: **Shoshin Society (Japan)**
Country: **USA**
Year: **1985**

U.S. designers were asked to create and contribute a poster to commemorate the bombing of Hiroshima. This poster encouraged reconciliation between the two giants (the US and the USSR symbolized by Godzilla and King Kong) that could destroy the world. It was part of the Images for Survival traveling exhibition and book as a gift to the Museum of Modern Art in Hiroshima, Japan. *(top left)*

Title: **A Fragile World**
Format: **Poster**
Art Director/Designer: **Ivan Chermayeff**
Client: **Shoshin Society (Japan)**
Country: **USA**
Year: **1985**

A classic idyllic image on an antique plate has been shattered. The plate, crudely taped back together, demonstrates the fragility of life and our world and how difficult it is to put things right again after they have gone wrong. *(top right)*

Title: **My Daughter's Hand**
Format: **Poster**
Art Director/Designer: **Tom Geismar**
Client: **Shoshin Society (Japan)**
Country: **USA**
Year: **1985**

This image of the designer's daughter's hand conveys both the idea of "peace" and "stop." The intrinsic lines and creases of the open palm also suggest the uniqueness and sanctity of each individual life. *(bottom)*

Title: **Victory**
Format: **Poster**
Art Director/Designer:
Fang Chen
Client: **No client**
Country: **USA**
Year: **1998**

This artist writes of his work, "The capitalized V represented by the two fingers is a universal symbol for victory and is understood by viewers of all races and cultures. According to Chinese folklore, the lines in human hands are not only records of the past but also foretell the future." In his work, these lines and the missing fingers also speak to the reality that human beings often experience suffering in order to achieve triumph.

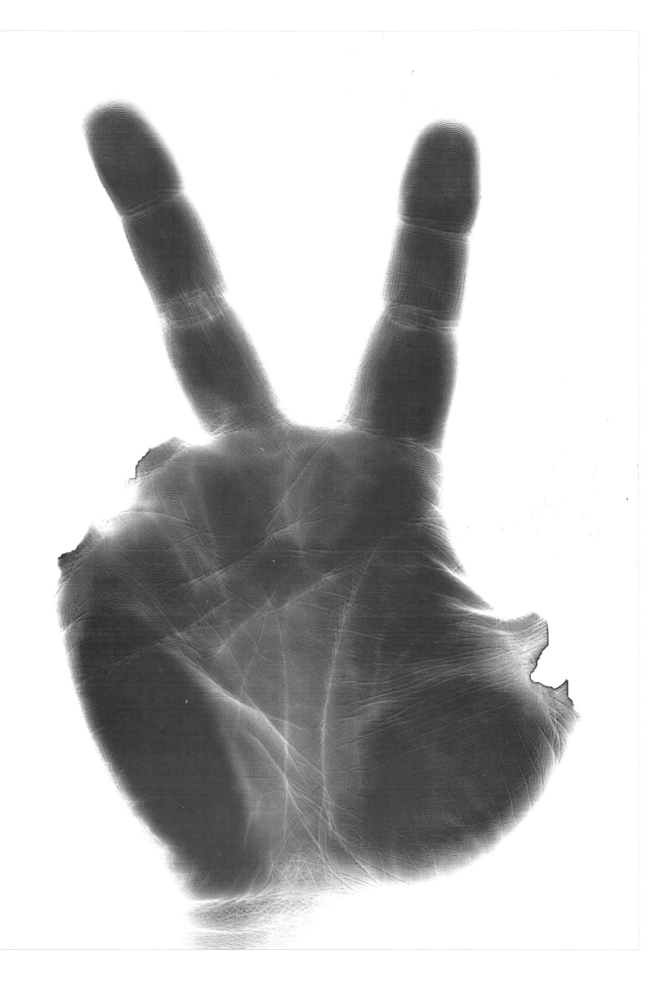

Title: **Racism**
Format: **Poster**
Art Director/Designer:
Cedomir Kostović
Client: **Southwest
Missouri State University**
Country: **USA**
Year: **1998**

Simple, poignant, and powerful, this image effectively illustrates the irrationality of racism.

Title: **howiloveya**
Format: **Poster**
Art Director/Designer:
Mark Fox
Client: **BlackDog**
Country: **USA**
Year: **1998**

This poster argues that
Mickey Mouse is a racist
figure based on a blackface
character.

Title: **Use Wyten to
Cover-up**
Format: **Magazine spread**
Art Director/Designers:
**Garth Walker,
Brandt Botes**
Client: *I-Jusi* **magazine**
Country: **South Africa**
Year: **1999**

I-Jusi (juice in Zulu) is
a free graphic design
magazine published in
Durban, South Africa. This
image was created for "The
Black & White" issue and is
a comment on an apartheid
era concept of black-
skinned people wanting to
appear more white. Skin
lighteners, which are
proven to be damaging to
the skin, are still employed
by many non-whites.

Title: **Laudium Welcomes Comrade Mandela**
Format: **Poster**
Art Director/Designer: **Unknown**
Client: **Unknown**
Country: **South Africa**
Year: **1990**

This poster welcoming Mandela for his visit to the township Laudium, and the ones to the right, were produced in the "old South Africa" and was therefore illegal under the terms of the "state of emergency." Posters of this nature are now virtually impossible to come by.

Title: **Happy Birthday Nelson Mandela**
Format: **Poster**
Art Director/Designer: **Unknown**
Client: **Mandela Birthday Committee, Cape Town**
Country: **South Africa**
Year: **1988**

Title: **Release Nelson Mandela**
Format: **Poster**
Art Director/Designer: **Surinder Singh**
Client: **Anti-Apartheid Movement**
Country: **South Africa**
Year: **1988**

These Anti-Apartheid posters from the 1980s demanded freedom for Nelson Mandela and also wished him a "happy 70th birthday" in prison. The government ban on Nelson Mandela's physical image contributed to the absence of compelling current photographs. *(top right)*

Title: **Make-up for Beginners**
Format: **Poster**
Art Director/Designer: **Joost Veerkamp**
Client: **Stichting Culture in Another South Africa, Amsterdam**
Country: **South Africa**
Year: **1987**

Pieter Willem Botha, the president of South Africa from 1984 to 1989, was forced to resign by his own party and was succeded by Frederik W. de Klerk who ultimately dismantled the apartheid system, holding free and fair elections. Here we see him being forcefully changed into Nelson Mandela. *(bottom)*

Title: **Article 4**
Article 15/Article 29
Format: **Poster**
Art Director/Designer:
Chaz Maviyane-Davies
Client: **No client**
Country: **USA**
Year: **1996**

These pieces were part of a
series of thirteen posters
based on the United
Nations Articles on Human
Rights as seen from the
African perspective.

No one should be subjected to slavery or servitude

Title: Volcano Type
Format: Typeface
Art Director/Designers:
Lars Harmsen,
Ulrich Weiß, Boris Kahl
Client: volcano-type.de
Country: Germany
Year: 2003/2004

More than 5,000 images of
Khmer Rouge victims from
the Tuol Sleng Prison in
Phnom Penh, the notorious
"S-21" extermination
center, make up the Yale
database located on the
Cambodian Genocide
Project website.
Photographs were taken of
prisoners being processed
into the facility for
interrogation and
execution. What shocked
the designer most about
those pictures was that "a
lot of the victims are
'nameless,' just a face with
a number. To create a 'font'
with these images was like
giving them an identity."

Title: natonalism
Format: Magazine ad
Art Director/Designers:
Aljoša Bagola,
Saša Dušan Leskovar
Client: *Mladina* magazine
Country: Slovenia
Year: 2003

This anti-NATO ad was
produced for the political
magazine *Mladina* at the
time when Slovenian
citizens held a referendum
to decide whether or not
they should accept their
invitation into NATO. The
designers draw attention to
the unilateral and agitating
role of the organization by
cropping NATO's own logo
in such a way as to liken it
to the Ku Klux Klan.

WATCHING

WAITING

Title: **Watching,
Waiting, Dreaming**
Format: **Poster series**
Art Director/Designer:
Robbie Conal
Client: **No client**
Country: **USA**
Year: **2002**

Three icons of nonviolent
activism are evoked in
this street-poster series
suggesting that the time
has come to act peacefully
in the world. Created in
reaction to the U.S.
government's aggressive
response to the tragedy of
September 11, these posters
depict Mahatma K. Gandhi
watching for peace, the
Dalai Lama waiting for the
return of his country, and
Martin Luther King, Jr.
dreaming of equality. It also
reminds us that there might
be alternatives to bombing.

DREAMING

Title: **Todos Los Hombres Somos Iguales?**
Format: **Poster**
Art Director/Designers: **Sonia Freeman, Gabriel Freeman**
Client: **Un Mundo Feliz/A Happy World Production**
Country: **Spain**

Part of the Ignorance = Intolerance project and inspired by the fiftieth anniversary of the Declaration of Human Rights, in 1998, this poster attempts to redefine conventional concepts of equality.

IGNORANCIA = INTOLERANCIA un mundo feliz / a happy world production

todos los hombres somos iguales?

Title: **Tout les homes sont égaux**
Format: **Poster**
Art Director/Designer:
Ebrahim Haghighi
Client: **No client**
Country: **Iran**
Year: **2003**

Totalitarianism inevitably produces cynicism and despair. This work proclaims "all men are equal" yet begets the observation that such equality only occurs after death.

Title: **I = U**
Format: **Poster**
Art Director/Designer:
Yarom Vardimon
Client: **ICU Publications**
Country: **Israel**
Year: **1999**

I = U, which is part of the designer's "graphic journalism" collection, calls for equality between races, men and women, and people everywhere. This "logo for equality" has been featured in exhibitions, museum shops, and international poster events.

Title: **Guilty Until Proven Innocent**
Format: **Various**
Art Director/Designer:
Araba Simpson
Client: **No client**
Country: **USA**
Year: **2004**

As shown here on their website, the School of Visual Arts MFA design students used a pushcart as the inspiration to "sell" ideas that included abuses of the justice system, a subversion on America's new identity control methods, and a stand that sells right-wing devotional images.

ARTISTS   ARABA SIMPSON

Mark Abrams
Cem Adiyaman
Julia Ames
Jared Barel
Celia Cheng
Rusty Clifton
Cecilia Guerrero
David Hartman
Kristopher Johns
Laura Kelly
Ishan Khosla
Sierra Krause
Juna Lee
Ed McKirdy
Anna Migirova
Lauren Monchik
Thomas Porostocky
Chris Ritchie
Jong Woo Si
Araba Simpson
Natalie Slocum
Kirsten Sorton
Johnathan Swafford
Emre Veryeri

Guilty Until Proven Innocent
The Guilty Until Proven Innocent cart is a commentary on the politics of the "justice" system. The cart highlights only a few of the hundreds--if not thousands-- of people who have been convicted, imprisoned, and then later found innocent of the crimes for which they were punished. Issues of race, gender, religion, and/or sexual-orientation play a role in these wrongful convictions.

SVA MFA DESIGN PRESENTS
PUSHCART
[THE ART OF PEDDLING]

EXHIBITION ARTISTS PHOTOS VIDEO PRESS CONTACT

Title: **Impunity,
Impossible Justice**
Format: **Poster**
Art Director/Designer:
Renato Aranda Rodríguez
Client: **No client**
Country: **Mexico**
Year: **2004**

By depicting a shackle that
cannot logically exist, this
poster protests the failure of
the Mexican criminal sys-
tem to punish corruption.

Title: **Born Suspect**
Format: **Poster**
Art Director/Designers:
Tom Sieu, John Givens
Client: **Amnesty
International**
Country: **USA**
Year: **2003**

Amnesty International
USA's Campaign Against
Discrimination
commissioned this poster
protesting racial profiling.
White cutout silhouettes
against a black background
emphasize the absurdity
and ineffectiveness of the
practice.

Title: **Human Rights Poster Series (Freedom of Opinion)**
Format: **Poster series**
Art Director/Designer: **Ethel Kessler**
Illustrator: **Geoffrey Moss**
Client: **United States Information Agency**
Country: **USA**
Year: **1978**

Article 19: Everyone has the right to freedom of opinion and expression; this right includes freedom to hold opinions without interference and to seek, receive, and impart information and ideas through any media and regardless of frontiers. *(top left)*

Title: **Human Rights Poster Series (On Recognition Before the Law)**
Format: **Poster**
Art Director/Designer: **Ethel Kessler**
Illustrator: **Alan E. Cober**
Client: **United States Information Agency**
Country: **USA**
Year: **1978**

Article 6: Everyone has the right to recognition everywhere as a person before the law. *(top right)*

Title: **Speak Up**
Format: **Poster**
Art Director/Designer: **Slavimir Stojanović**
Client: **Human Rights Council Belgrade**
Country: **Slovenia**
Year: **1996**

This poster illustrates the struggle for the freedom of speech with this dark, hand-drawn illustration. The strong typographical treatment adds to the power of the piece. *(bottom)*

Title: **No Comment**
Format: **Poster**
Art Director/Designer:
Jan Nuckowski
Client: **No client**
Country: **Poland**
Year: **1984**

This poster was created at a time when books and ideas were forbidden, "Truth—where there was light—was imprisoned behind iron bars," in the Iron Curtain countries. The only books and ideas that were allowed, at that time, were ones that were not considered "dangerous" by the government. (*top left*)

no comment

[first & last impression]   stop the police torture!

Title: **First & Last Impression**
Format: **Poster**
Art Director/Designer:
Tomato Košir
Mentor: **Zoravko Papič**
Client: **Amnesty International**
Country: **Slovenia**
Year: **2000**

One of a series of posters for Amnesty International, this chilling combination of words and an immediate image protests against police brutality and misconduct. Unfortunately, Amnesty International rejected the series. (*top right*)

Title: **Human Rights Artis 89**
Format: **Poster**
Art Director/Designer:
Rico Lins
Photographers: **Rico Lins, Katherine McGlynn**
Client: **Artis 89**
Country: **Brazil**
Year: **1989**

This poster was designed for an international event that invited 66 designers to participate in an exhibition and conference commemorating the 200th anniversary of the French Revolution in Paris. Artists were requested to depict or comment on the Human Rights Bill in their posters. This piece poses questions: 'Is this man the manipulator in his game; or is it he who, in fact, is being manipulated"? (*bottom*)

Title: **Caution: Children at War**
Format: **Poster**
Art Director/Designer: **Woody Pirtle/Pentagram**
Client: **Amnesty International**
Country: **USA**
Year: **1999**

Road signs are frequently used as a reference in protest, perhaps because the goal of the design is clear and immediate communication, and they are universally understood.

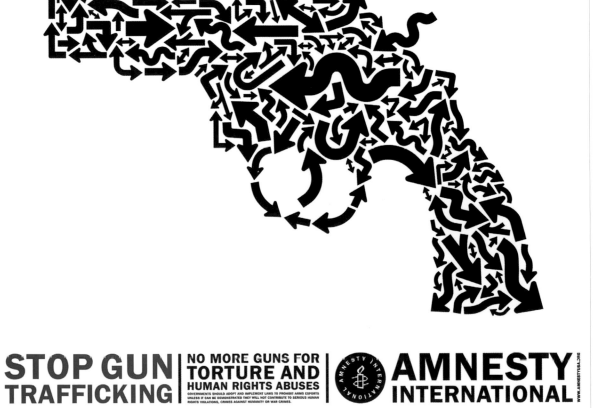

Title: **Stop Gun Trafficking**
Format: **Poster**
Art Director/Designer: **Woody Pirtle/Pentagram**
Client: **Amnesty International**
Country: **USA**
Year: **2001**

In July 2001, the United Nations held a conference on the illicit trade of small arms and light weapons. This image cleverly demonstrates the convoluted path that guns travel to get into the hands of their users.

FACE THE MUSIC | NGAWANG CHOEPHEL |

IS A TIBETAN MUSICIAN AND FULBRIGHT SCHOLAR.
CHINESE AUTHORITIES ARRESTED HIM IN 1995.

HIS "CRIME": DOCUMENTING TRADITIONAL TIBETAN MUSIC AND DANCE. HIS PUNISHMENT: 18 YEARS IN PRISON.

AMNESTY INTERNATIONAL

JOIN THE CAMPAIGN FOR NGAWANG CHOEPHEL'S RELEASE. VISIT WWW.AMNESTYUSA.ORG

Title: **Face the Music**
Format: **Poster**
Art Director/Designer:
Woody Pirtle/Pentagram
Client: **Amnesty International**
Country: **USA**
Year: **2000**

Ngawang Choephel is a Tibetan musician, scholar, and exile who was arrested by the Chinese authorities in 1995. The case was taken up by the Amnesty's "Artists for Amnesty" group and Choephel's release was obtained in January 2002 after Annie Lennox and many other international public figures participated in the campaign.

Title: **Universal Declaration of Human Rights**
Format: **Poster series**
Art Director/Designer: **Woody Pirtle/Pentagram**
Client: **Amnesty International**
Country: **USA**
Year: **2002**

Working with Amnesty International, the designer created a handsome and rational series of posters that spotlight twelve of the Universal Declaration of Human Rights (UDHR) individual articles. Adopted by the member states of the United Nations in 1948, the UDHR consists of thirty articles, which set out the human rights fundamental to the dignity and development of every human being. Amnesty International uses the declaration as the foundation of its activities. The posters were distributed to schools as part of the group's "Amnesty Educate" initiative, and a teacher's guide was created containing lesson plans for each of the twelve posters. The intent was to make the UDHR into a living and memorable document that students could relate to.

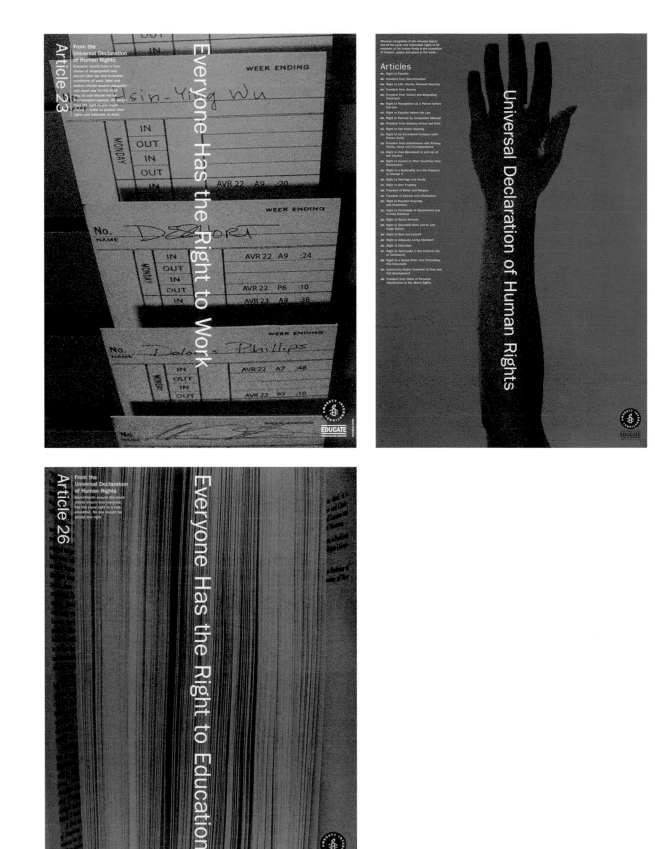

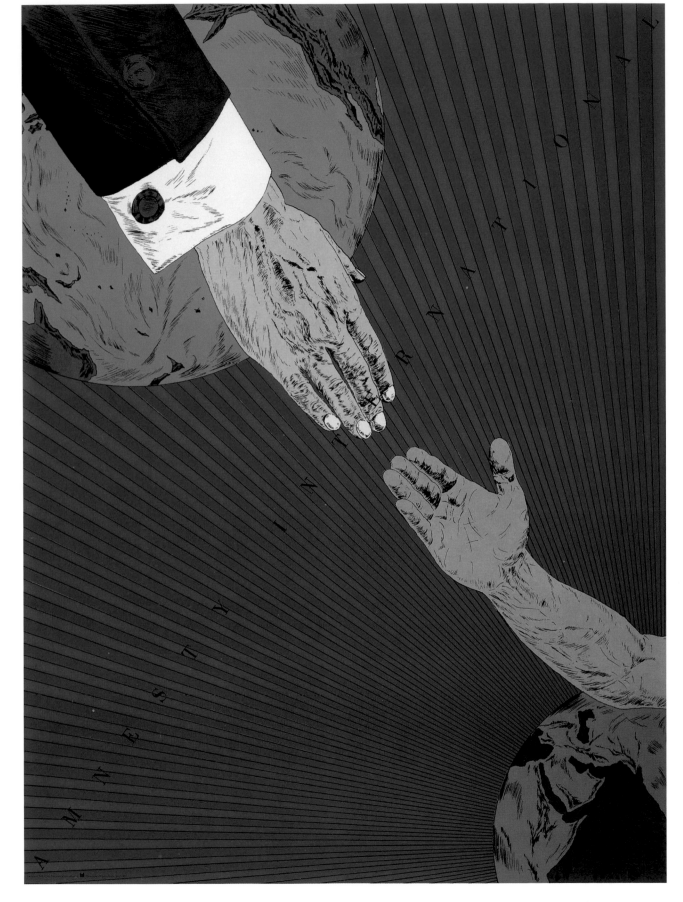

Title: **Amnesty International**
Format: **Poster**
Art Director/Designer:
Tadanori Yokoo
Client: **Amnesty International**
Country: **Japan**
Year: **1976**

One can clearly see the influence of Ukiyo-e prints on this image illustrating humans reaching out to political prisoners. This poster was commissioned by Amnesty International's New York office.

Title: **Poster Against Xenophoby**
Format: **Poster**
Art Director/Designers: **Sonia Freeman, Gabriel Freeman**
Client: **Istituto Europeo di Design**
Country: **Spain**
Year: **2002**

The handprint illustrates the stupidity of xenophobia in a world made up of mixed blood. The poster was created for a themed exhibition on "half-bred people" at the IED (Istituto Europeo di Design) in Madrid. (*top left*)

Title: **Poster Against Torture**
Format: **Poster**
Art Director/Designers: **Sonia Freeman, Gabriel Freeman**
Client: **Un Mundo Feliz/A Happy World Production**
Country: **Spain**
Year: **2001**

The clean, simple style of this illustration reinforces the message that torture is not confined to any particular political system; it occurs in democracies as well as dictatorships and under civilian, as well as military governments. The work was distributed free over the Internet. (*top right*)

Title: **Bolted Hands**
Format: **Poster**
Art Director/Designer: **Lanny Sommese**
Client: **Amnesty International chapter at Penn State University**
Country: **USA**
Year: **1981**

This dynamic poster for Amnesty International was designed to raise awareness about the torture that humans continually inflict upon one another and to remind viewers of Amnesty's mission. The visceral drip drawing style of the praying hands was used to contrast the mechanically drawn bolt and heighten the emotional impact of the image. The bolt and hands were then scaled and juxtaposed to appear as a cross "to make the image more emblematic." (*bottom*)

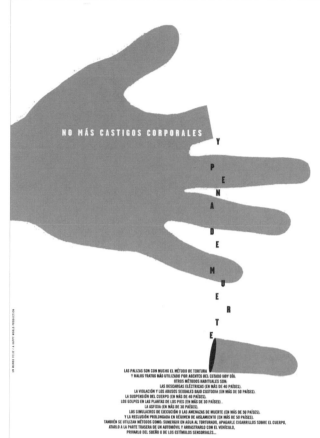

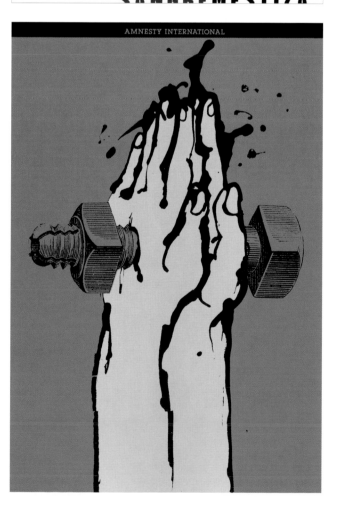

HUMAN TRAFFICKING IS MODERN-DAY SLAVERY

Title: **Human Trafficking Is Modern-Day Slavery**
Format: **Poster**
Art Director/Designers:
**Alex Briseno,
Hernan Ibanez**
Client: **Florida Freedom
Partnership**
Country: **USA**
Year: **2004**

Florida Freedom Partnership is a federally funded, non-profit organization offering comprehensive services to victims of human trafficking or modern day slavery. This poster is part of an outreach campaign designed to educate the public on the problem of human trafficking and to urge victims to seek protection and support from the organization.

Men, women and children in our community are forced to work against their will in the sex industry, restaurants, hotels, agricultural work, sweat-shops, and domestic servitude. Safe housing, interpretation, legal and medical services are available to victims, but first they must be found.

LET THE TRUTH **COME OUT**

If you or someone you know is a
victim of modern-day slavery, call:

1-866-443-0106

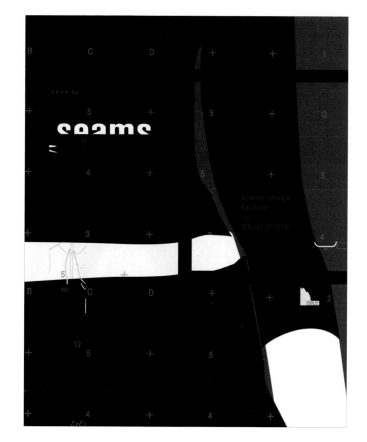

Title: **Seams: Media Design, Fashion, and Social Justice**
Format: **Garment**
Art Director/Designer: **Adriana Parcero**
Client: **No client**
Country: **USA**
Year: **2003**

In its aim to raise awareness about the often harsh realities of the garment industry, Seams uses clothing as a vehicle to comment on sweatshops, making visible and wearable the information little known to consumers. In addition, their high-end fashion catalog has been turned into a political manifesto, and the designer has created a website (seams.la) so the work and message can reach a wider audience.

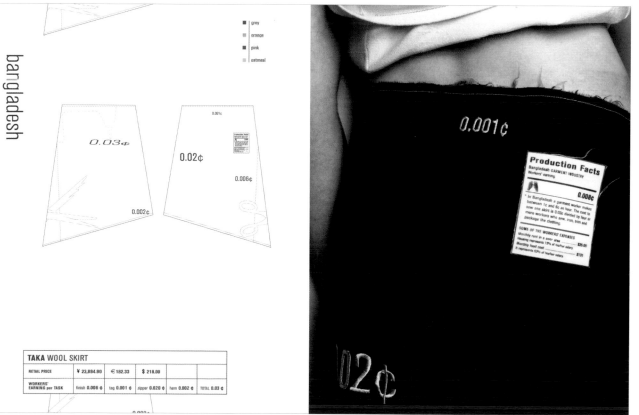

Title: **Printed In USA**
Format: **Poster**
Art Director/Designer:
Emek
Client: **Public Campaign**
Country: **USA**
Year: **2003**

Fingerprints in America
have become equivalent
to barcodes, making people
easier to monitor.
For exactly that reason,
U.S. customs is now
fingerprinting every foreign
visitor who enters the
country.

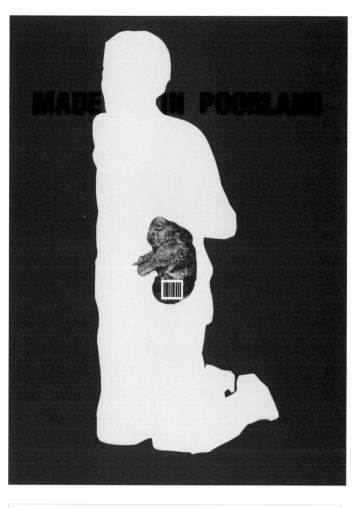

Title: **Made In Poorland**
Format: **Poster**
Art Director/Designer:
Jarek Bujny
Client: **No client**
Country: **Poland**
Year: **2003**

The UPC tag on the kidney tells us the poor and powerless exist as "parts." The international market for organs has stripped them of their rights, needs, and culture as human beings.

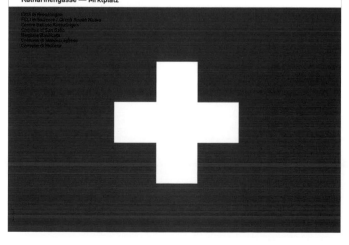

Title: **Emigrazione**
Format: **Poster**
Art Director/Designer:
Mauro Bubbico
Client: **Associaz Emigranti Svizzera**
Country: **Italy**
Year: **2000**

This poster commemorates the 50th anniversary of a 1949 peasant rebellion in southern Italy that resulted in significant Italian immigration to Switzerland. The work comments on the fact that many political rights and the opportunity to become full Swiss citizens are still denied to immigrants.

THE *AMERICAN*™ *DREAM*

DEVIL MAY CARE

Title: **Devil May Care**
Format: **Poster**
Art Director/Designer:
Jeff Louviere
Client: **The American**™
Dream
Country: **USA**
Year: **2002**

The consequences of the laissez-faire spirit of New Orleans is revealed by an image of legendary stunt man, Evil Knievel moto-vaulting over a long line of degraded and exploited dark skinned men. The designer created this poster in response to the lack of social commentary in New Orleans, and posted them around the city in the middle of the night.

Title: **Migranti Diritti e Pace**
Format: **Poster**
Art Director/Designer: **Mauro Bubbico**
Client: **Social Forum Matera**
Country: **Italy**
Year: **Unknown**

The dark-skinned model holds a target to make clear the xenophobic racist consequences on immigrants on this poster protesting a new discriminatory Italian immigration law.

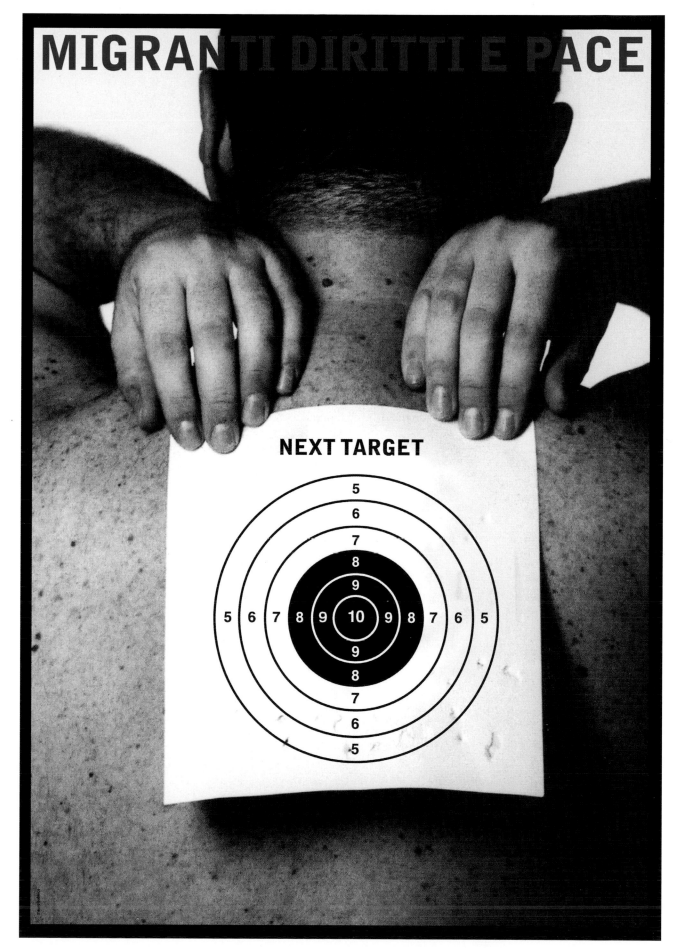

MIGRANTI DIRITTI E PACE

NEXT TARGET

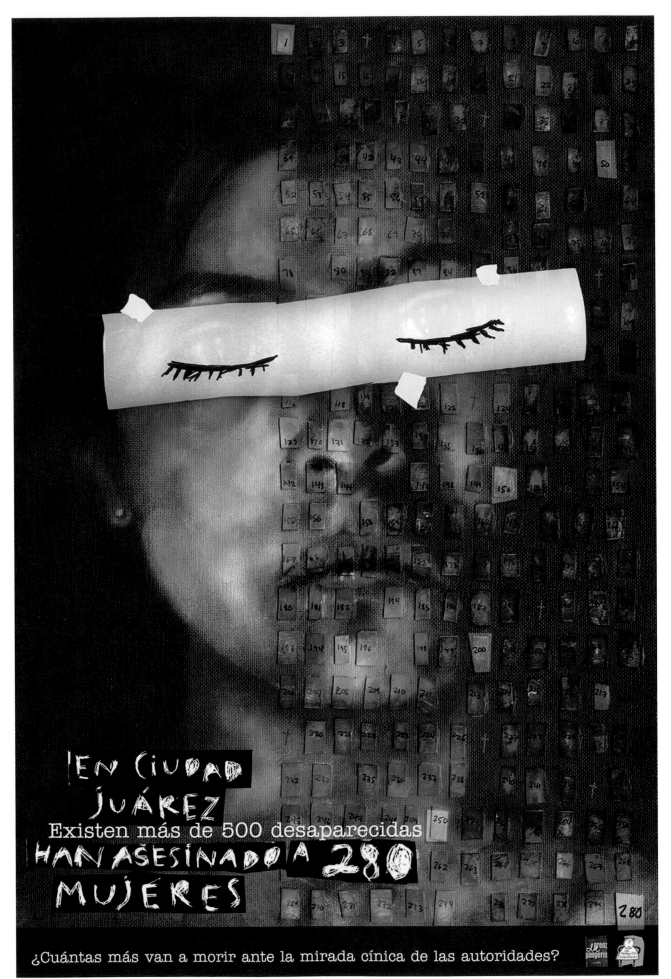

Title: **More Than 280 Women Have Been Murdered**
Format: **Poster**
Art Director/Designer: **Margarita Sada**
Client: **Die Gresgangerin**
Country: **Mexico**
Year: **2002**

The designer notes "For more than ten years, hundreds of women in the Mexican town of Juarez have been kidnapped, raped, murdered, and grotesquely maimed. After years of official apathy and police incompetence toward solving and ending these brutal murders, the families of the missing women started actions to demand justice. I made this poster to support their stuggle." The text reads "More than 280 women have been murdered in Juárez City and another 500 more are missing. How many more are going to die under the cynical stare of authorities?"

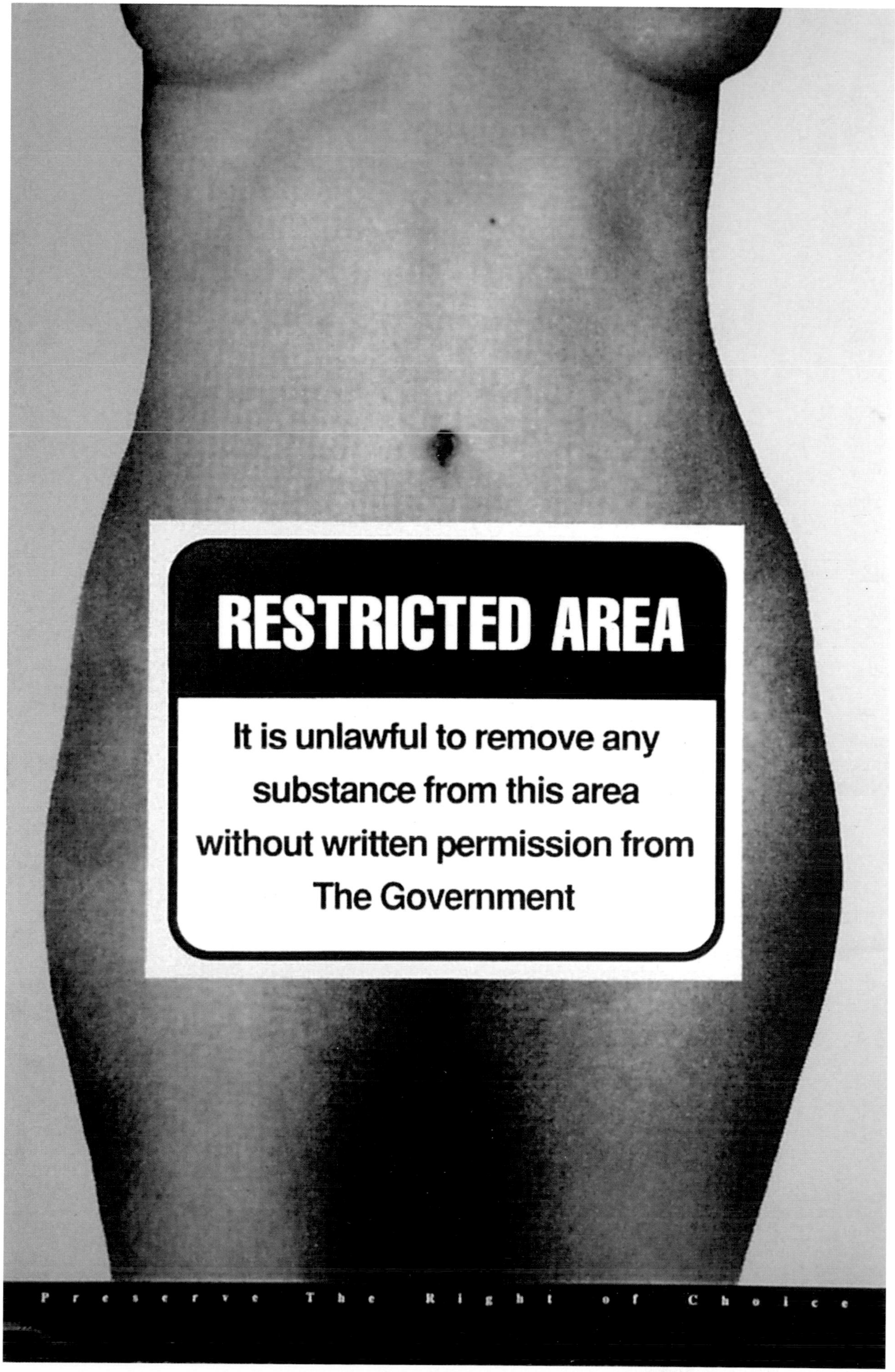

Title: **Preserve the Right of Choice**
Format: **Poster**
Art Director/Designer:
Trudy Cole-Zielanski
Client: **No client**
Country: **USA**
Year: **1993**

"This poster was designed to promote the understanding that a woman's body is her own, and she has the ultimate right to say what she does with it."

RESTRICTED AREA

It is unlawful to remove any substance from this area without written permission from The Government

Preserve The Right of Choice

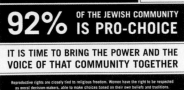

NCJW'S VOICE:
THE VOICE OF THE JEWISH COMMUNITY

FOR OVER A CENTURY THE NATIONAL COUNCIL OF JEWISH WOMEN HAS BEEN AT THE FOREFRONT OF SOCIAL CHANGE—COURAGEOUSLY TAKING A PROGRESSIVE STANCE ON ISSUES SUCH AS REPRODUCTIVE FREEDOM. TODAY, NCJW IS THE LEADING JEWISH ORGANIZATION FIGHTING TO PROTECT THAT FREEDOM.

As Jews, we understand what it means to have fundamental rights and liberties stripped away.

WE CANNOT BE SILENT ON THIS ISSUE

92% OF THE JEWISH COMMUNITY IS PRO-CHOICE

IT IS TIME TO BRING THE POWER AND THE VOICE OF THAT COMMUNITY TOGETHER

Reproductive rights are closely tied to religious freedom. Women have the right to be respected as moral decision-makers, able to make choices based on their own beliefs and traditions. For the courts to impose one religion's view on all of us defies the very meaning of religious liberty.

NCJW'S BENCHMARK CAMPAIGN IS ALREADY TAKING ACTION:

EDUCATING AND MOBILIZING THOUSANDS OF PEOPLE

LEADING PRO-CHOICE RALLIES AND COMMUNITY EVENTS ACROSS THE COUNTRY

BUILDING STATE COALITIONS

FLYING KEY LEADERS AND SPEAKERS TO WASHINGTON, DC TO MEET WITH SENATORS

EMPOWERING ONLINE ACTIVISTS VIA ALERTS, UPDATES, AND AN INTERACTIVE WEB SITE

NOW, IT'S YOUR TURN
LOG ON TO WWW.BENCHMARKCAMPAIGN.ORG AND JOIN BENCHMARK TODAY

Title: **It's About Time**
Format: **Brochure**
Art Director/Designers:
**David Schimmel,
Susan Brzozowski**
Client: **National Council
of Jewish Women**
Country: **USA**
Year: **2004**

Serving as both a wake up call and a call to action, this booklet informs readers of the threats facing Roe vs. Wade and urges them to protect their right to safe, legal abortion by contacting their senators.

BENCHMARK, THE NATIONAL COUNCIL OF JEWISH WOMEN'S CAMPAIGN TO SAVE ROE EDUCATES, MOBILIZES, AND ADVOCATES— REACHING OUT TO THE DECISION-MAKERS IN WASHINGTON, DC TO DELIVER YOUR VOICE ON THE IMPORTANCE OF FUNDAMENTAL FREEDOMS, INCLUDING WOMEN'S RIGHT TO REPRODUCTIVE CHOICE.

The right to make independent childbearing decisions has enabled women to pursue educational and employment opportunities that were unthinkable a generation ago.

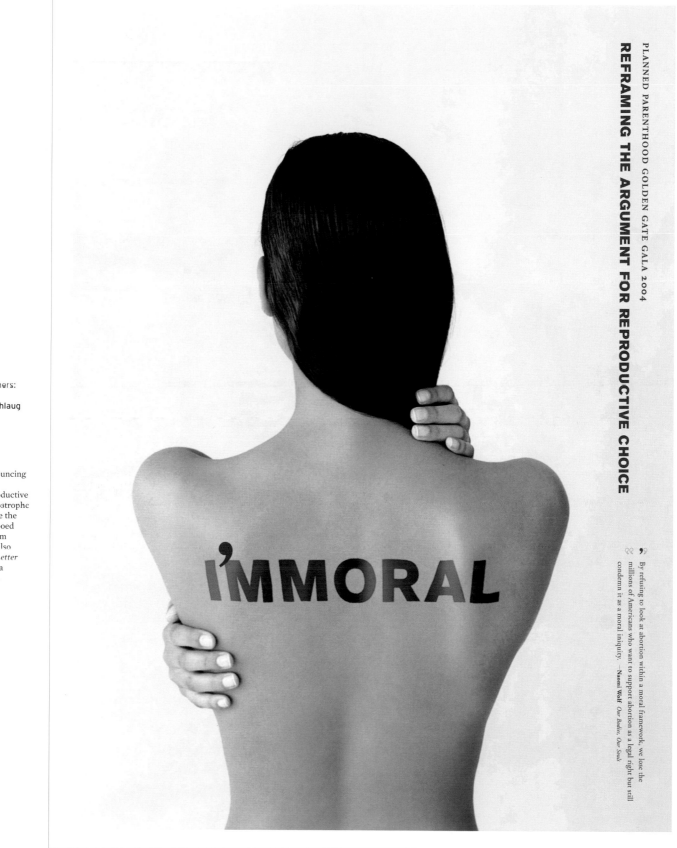

Title: **I'mmoral**
Format: **Poster**
Art Director/Designers:
**AddisGroup–John
Creson, Monica Schlaug**
Client: **Planned
Parenthood**
Country: **USA**
Year: **2004**

For this poster announcing
the "Reframing the
Argument for Reproductive
Choice" gala, an apostrophe
was added to change the
meaning of the tattooed
word immoral to "I'm
moral." The image also
evokes *The Scarlet Letter*
and the pain felt by a
stigmatized woman.

PLANNED PARENTHOOD GOLDEN GATE GALA 2004

REFRAMING THE ARGUMENT FOR REPRODUCTIVE CHOICE

By refusing to look at abortion within a moral framework, we lose the millions of Americans who want to support abortion as a legal right but still condemn it as a moral iniquity. —*Naomi Wolf, Our Bodies, Our Souls*

Title: **Ethiopia**
Planned Parenthood
Format: **Poster**
Art Director/Designers:
Nancy Hoefig,
Monica Schlaug
Client: **Planned**
Parenthood
Country: **USA**
Year: **2001**

An alliance between
Planned Parenthood and
its Ethiopian counterpart
neatly refers to the goal
of successful birth
control access by cleverly
using various types of
contraception to construct
an African-inspired mask
for a gala invitation.

PRICE OF LIFE

The dowry, once a gift from the bride's family to the groom's in arranged marriages, has become little more than a form of extortion. More than 5,000 Indian women die each year from dowry deaths and suicides because their in-laws consider their dowries inadequate. Help abolish the dowry system and stop the sale of women.

www.stopdowry.org

Title: **Price of Life**
Format: **Poster**
Art Director/Designer:
Wishmini Perera
Client: **No client**
Country: **USA**
Year: **2003**

In this poster, done for a class assignment, traditional bridal decorations are used to oppose the dowry system practiced in South Asia. The hand is held up as if to say "Stop!"

Title: **Sri Lanka**
Format: **Postcard**
Art Director/Designer:
Chaz Maviyane-Davies
Client: **No client**
Country: **USA**
Year: **2002**

This is a commentary on former Sri Lankan Prime Minister Ratnasiri Wickremanayake's speech in which he urged the country to support war efforts by having more babies to swell the ranks of the army and vanquish separatist Tamil Tiger rebels.

Sri Lanka's Prime Minister Ratnasiri Wickremanayake has urged the country to support war efforts by having more babies to help swell the ranks of the army and vanquish separatist Tamil Tiger rebels... June 2001

Title: **Crucified Woman**
Format: **Illustration**
Illustrator: **Eric Drooker**
Client: *The Village Voice*
Country: **USA**
Year: **1991**

This image of a woman, prosecuted through the centuries by the hands of governments and religious leaders, has become a popular icon and tattoo design among feminists internationally. *(top left)*

Title: **Freedom for Women Political Prisoners**
Format: **Poster**
Art Director/Designer: **Margarita Sada**
Client: **No client**
Country: **Mexico**
Year: **1999**

In 1999, the students of the National University in Mexico City went on strike to demand the democratization of political institutions. The strike lasted ten months, ending when the police broke in and imprisoned hundreds of students, many of whom were girls. The text reads: "Freedom for Women Political Prisoners. March 8th International Day of Women. Lots of Girls. We are bad and we can be worse." *(top right)*

Title: **Republicans Against Choice**
Format: **Illustration**
Illustrator: **Frances Jetter**
Client: **Davidson Galleries**
Country: **USA**
Year: **1992**

The similarity between the appearance of an elephant (Republican symbol) head and a woman's reproductive organs was used to comment on the republican party's position on abortion. Originally commissioned and then refused by the *New York Times* op-ed pages, it was eventually published by *The Village Voice* and then printed on T-shirts. *(bottom)*

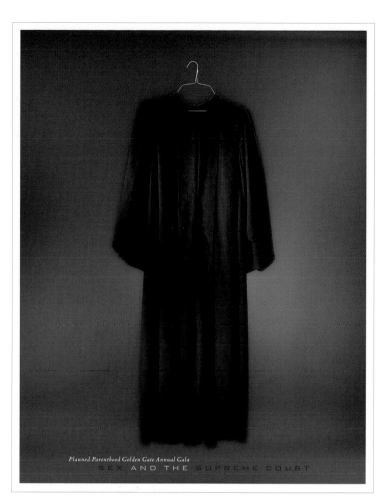

Title: **Sex and the Supreme Court**
Format: **Poster**
Art Director/Designer:
Joanne Hom
Client: **Planned Parenthood**
Country: **USA**
Year: **2003**

This ominous reference to coat-hanger abortions is used as an effective graphic warning on an invitation to a Planned Parenthood fundraiser.

Title: **Class Action**
Format: **T-shirts**
Art Director/Designers:
**Rodney Abbot,
Debra Drovillo,
Lisa Mangano,
Alexandra Min,
Louise Scovell,
Lisa Shoglow**
Client: **No client**
Country: **USA**
Year: **1992**

A small collective of graduate students at Yale joined forces to raise awareness of the issue of protecting a woman's right to choose. This T-shirt illustrates the conflict between those who believe that abortion is an individual decision as protected by the Roe v. Wade decision and those who feel it is something that should be decided by government.

Title: **Class Action**
Format: **Billboard**
Art Director/Designers:
**Rodney Abbot,
Debra Drovillo,
Lisa Mangano,
Alexandra Min,
Louise Scovell,
Lisa Shoglow**
Client: **No client**
Country: **USA**
Year: **1992**

This pro-choice message was produced as a billboard situated prominently on the highly trafficked route I-95 in Connecticut.

Title: **The Anatomically Correct Oscar**
Format: **Billboard**
Art Director/Designer:
Guerrilla Girls, Inc.
Client: **No client**
Country: **USA**
Year: **2001**

"The anatomically correct Oscar: He's white & male, just like the guys who win!" This billboard, sponsored by the Guerrilla Girls, was displayed a few blocks away from the Academy Awards ceremony to point out the sexism and racism that's rampant in the film industry.

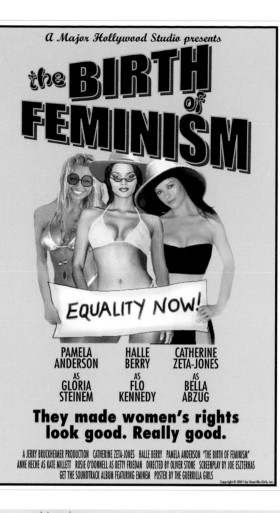

Title: **The Birth of Feminism**
Format: **Poster**
Art Director/Designer: **Guerrilla Girls, Inc.**
Client: **No client**
Country: **USA**
Year: **2001**

This parody of a major Hollywood studio poster features well-known actresses portraying three of the most important U.S. feminist activists of recent times in their signature looks. Pink sunglasses and a cowboy hat were Kennedy's trademarks, Abzug favored dramatic headwear, and Steinem is known for her large glasses.

Title: **Do Women Have to Be Naked to Get into the Met. Museum?**
Format: **Poster**
Art Director/Designer: **Guerrilla Girls, Inc.**
Client: **No client**
Country: **USA**
Year: **1989**

Since 1985, the Guerrilla Girls, a bunch of anonymous females who take the names of dead women artists as pseudonyms and appear in public wearing gorilla masks, have produced more than one hundred posters, stickers, books, printed projects, and actions that expose sexism and racism in politics, the art world, film, and the culture at large. This poster protests the lack of female artists in the Metropolitan Museum of Art and questions "Do women have to be naked to get into the Met Museum?"

Do women have to be naked to get into the Met. Museum?

Less than 5% of the **artists** in the Modern Art sections are women, but 85% of the **nudes** are female.

GUERRILLA GIRLS CONSCIENCE OF THE ART WORLD
w w w . g u e r r i l l a g i r l s . c o m

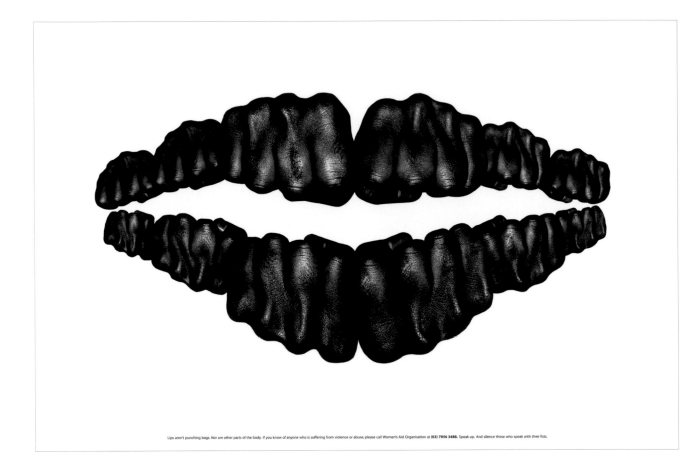

Lips aren't punching bags. Nor are other parts of the body. If you know of anyone who is suffering from violence or abuse, please call Women's Aid Organisation at (03) 7956 3488. Speak up. And silence those who speak with their fists.

Title: **Shattered, Fists & Figures**
Format: **Unknown**
Art Director/Designer: **Theresa Tsang Teng**
Client: **Woman's Aid Organization (WAO)**
Country: **Malaysia**
Year: **Unknown**

Upon first glance these three illustrations for a woman's aid organization fighting domestic abuse appear as beautiful female lips. Upon closer inspection they reveal fists, men beating women, and broken glass, lending them an element of surprise and impact.

Silent lips mute the sound of beatings. And muzzle unspeakable pain. Give voice to victims of violence or abuse. Please call Women's Aid Organisation at (03) 7956 3488. Deep as the wounds may be, healing begins by being heard.

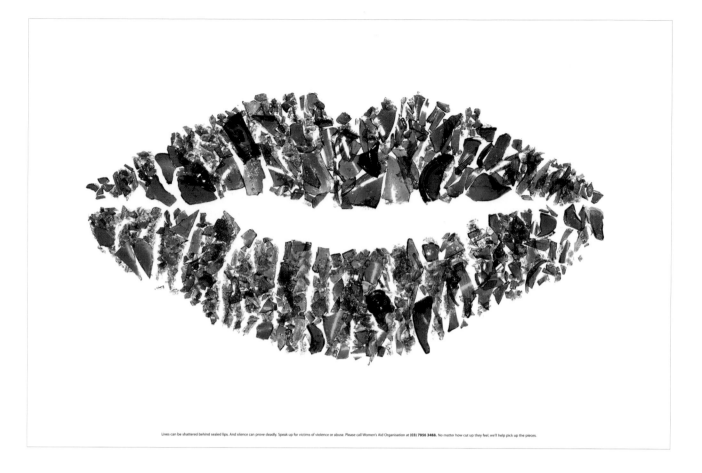

Lives can be shattered behind sealed lips. And silence can prove deadly. Speak up for victims of violence or abuse. Please call Women's Aid Organisation at **(03) 7956 3488.** No matter how cut up they feel, we'll help pick up the pieces.

Title: **Women Against Rape (WAR)**
Format: **Logo**
Art Director/Designer: **Carole Goodson**
Client: **Women Against Rape (WAR)**
Country: **USA**
Year: **1972**

This clever acronym for a grassroots women's group, which mobilized in response to an increase in violence against women, is immediate and powerful.

Title: **Musical Expressions**
Format: **Poster series**
Art Director/Designers:
**Tan Kien Eng,
Theresa Tsang Teng**
Client: **Women's Aid
Organization (WAO)**
Country: **Malaysia**
Year: **Unknown**

A series of posters
promoting a benefit concert
whose proceeds went to
Women's Aid Organization
to help fight gender
violence.

DON'T wear make-up.

Don't wear your hair long.

Don't wear short skirts.

Don't wear high heels.

Don't wear tight-fitting clothes.

Don't look sexy.

Don't bat your eyelashes.

Don't crack dirty jokes.

Don't flirt.

Don't smile at strangers.

Don't offer help to strangers.

Don't go out at night.

Don't go to parties.

Don't go on dates.

Don't go anywhere alone.

Don't attract attention.

Don't work late.

Don't trust anyone.

Don't say yes.

Don't say no.

Don't be a woman.

Don't exist.

Do call Women's Aid Organisation at 03-7956 3488 to help stop prejudice and violence against women. You can make a difference.

Title: **Don't**
Format: **Poster**
Art Director/Designer:
Tan Kien Eng
Client: **Women's Aid Organization (WAO)**
Country: **Malaysia**
Year: **Unknown**

This poster rebuffs a campaign to discourage violence against Malaysian women by urging modesty. Here, the designer opposes this concept through irony and the punch line "don't exist."

Title: **Front Page**
Format: **Flipbook**
Art Director/Designer:
Dušan Petričić
Client:
Galleria Graficki Kolektiv
Country: **Yugoslavia**
Year: **1971**

This privately published catalogue-flipbook from Communist Yugoslavia shows the human need for freedom and self-expression. (*far right and following pages*)

Title: **Search and Destroy**
Format: **Magazine cover**
Art Director/Designer:
Scott Stowell
Client: *The Nation*
Country: **USA**
Year: **2000**

This cover addresses the
U.S. military's intolerance
of homosexuality and their
"don't ask, don't tell" policy
by covering the classic ACT
UP "silence = death" pink
triangle with camouflage.

Title: **Gay Teen Suicide**
Format: **Poster**
Art Director/Designers:
**Sean Adams,
Ashton Taylor**
Photographer: **Blake Little**
Client: **World Studio
Foundation**
Country: **USA**
Year: **2003**

This poster was designed to
promote awareness of the
disproportionally high
occurrence of suicide
among gay teenagers.

NEW PALTZ • NEW YORK • 2004

I DO!

SUPPORT SAME-SEX MARRIAGE, MAYOR JASON WEST, REVEREND KAY GREENLEAF & REVEREND DAWN SANGREY

DESIGN: JEFF FISHER LOGOMOTIVES © 2004

Title: **I DO!**
Format: **Poster**
Art Director/Designer: **Jeff Fisher**
Client: **No client**
Country: **USA**
Year: **2004**

After a public backlash to same-sex marriage licenses being issued in Multnomah County, Oregon, this designer created the "I DO!" image and distributed it via email for use by those supporting the legalization of same-sex marriage. Flyers, stickers, and buttons were produced and displayed in the windows of businesses and homes, on the bumpers of cars, and at public hearings on the topic. Similar items were also designed for campaigns in California, Massachusetts, New York, and New Mexico.

Title: **LGBT Marriage and Family**
Format: **Brochure**
Art Director/Designer: **Mirko Ilić**
Client: **MLGBA (Massachusetts Lesbian and Gay Bar Association)**
Country: **USA**
Year: **2004**

This illustration originally appeared in the *Village Voice*, a New York free newspaper, accompanying a story on gay marriage. It caught the eye of the Massachusetts Lesbian and Gay Bar Association, who now use it on the covers of their informational brochures that outline how marriage will affect individual's rights and benefits. The image was inspired by the famous picture *V-J Day, The Kiss*, taken in 1945 by Alfred Eisenstaedt, in which a sailor is kissing a nurse in Times Square on Victory in Japan Day.

LGBT Marriage and Family

Legal Resources

Sponsored by
the Massachusetts
Lesbian and Gay
Bar Association
Family Law
Section

So, are you two gonna get married?

What You Need to Know

Sponsored by
the Massachusetts
Lesbian and Gay
Bar Association
Family Law
Section

Title: **AIDS!**
Format: **Poster**
Art Director/Designer:
Fang Chen
Client: **No client**
Country: **USA**
Year: **2003**

The war against AIDS is literally depicted in this poster promoting awareness. The helmet, used as a visual metaphor, reminds us that war has its casualties but perhaps this image's strength lies in its deliberate provocation to discuss a subject too often ignored.

Old Glory condoms and T-shirts, for ordering information call
1-800-726-1930
in Massachusetts call 508.487-1930
10 A.M. - 4 P.M. E.S.T., Mon.-Fri.
order form enclosed

Old Glory Pledge
We believe it is patriotic to protect and save lives. We offer only the highest quality condoms. Join us in promoting safer sex. Help eliminate AIDS.

A portion of Old Glory profits will be donated to AIDS related services.

**Old Glory Condom Corporation
Provincetown, MA 02657
Made in U.S.A.**

This product combines a latex condom and a spermicidal lubricant. The spermicide nonoxynol-9 reduces the number of active sperm thereby decreasing the risk of pregnancy if you lose your erection before withdrawal and some semen spill outside the condom. However, the extent of decreased risk has not been established. This condom should not be used as a substitute for the combined use of a vaginal spermicide and a condom.

Title: **Old Glory Condoms**
Format: **Condom packaging**
Art Director/Designers:
**Judy Kohn,
Kohn Kruikshank**
Client: **Old Glory Condom Corp.**
Country: **USA**
Year: **1989**

In 1989, the government was challenged to redefine patriotism after the Supreme Court decision protecting flag-burning under the First Amendment was enacted. The U.S. Department of Commerce refused a trademark, during the height of the AIDS epidemic, saying it was "immoral and scandalous" to associate the flag with sex. Three years later, the name and image were finally granted trademark protections.

Title: **Copriti**
Format: **Poster**
Art Director/Designer:
Mauro Bubbico
Client: **AIAP**
Country: **Italy**
Year: **Unknown**

This poster asks viewers to "cover-up" so as not to be surprised by AIDS.

NON FARTI SORPRENDERE DALL'AIDS COPRITI

Human Resources are limited. What should be done with it, to live or to fight?

Title: **Human Resources**
Format: **Poster**
Art Director/Designer:
Tahamtan Aminian
Client: **Fioreh Publication**
Country: **Iran**
Year: **2002**

Gunnysacks can be
employed to hold flour,
used in creating life-
sustaining bread, or as
sandbags, used to erect the
trenches of war. This poster
acknowledges that we have
limited resources and asks
if we will use them "to live
or to fight."

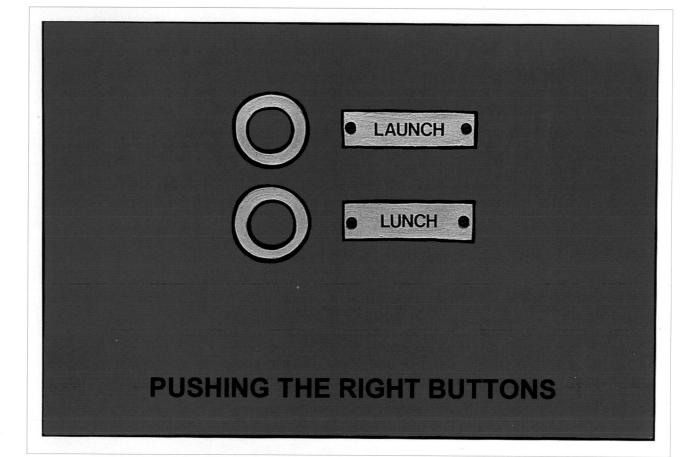

Title: **Pushing
the Right Buttons**
Format: **Illustration**
Art Director/Designer:
Erika Rothenberg
Client: **No client**
Country: **USA**
Year: **1982**

The political choice
between feeding the
hungry or military
aggression is dramatized
in this poster.

Title: **Over 17,000,000
Ukrainians Are Living
Below the Poverty Line**
Format: **Poster**
Art Director/Designer:
Anatoliy Omelchenko
Client: **Private Bank**
Country: **USA**
Year: **2000**

The text reading "Over
17,000,000 Ukrainians
Are Living Below the
Poverty Line" is simply and
effectively illustrated with
the familiar graphic
admonishment to properly
dispose of trash. Items
casually discarding by one
are all too often desperately
searched for by another, in
an effort to survive.

Понад 17,000,000 українців живуть за межею бідності.

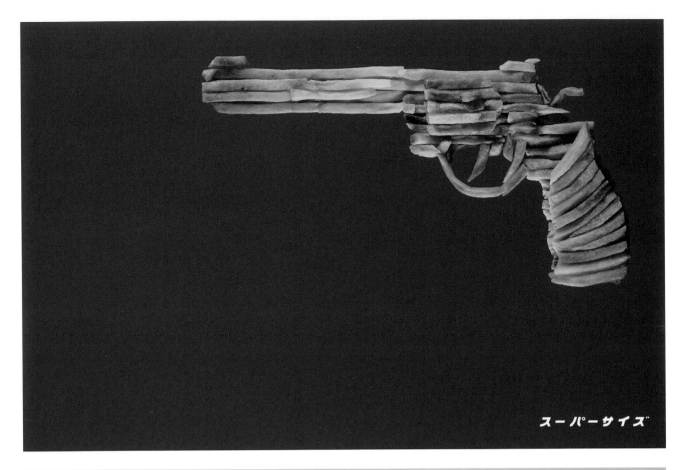

スーパーサイズ™

Title: **Supersize**
Format: **Magazine spread**
Creative Directors:
**Joshua Berger,
Niko Courtelis,
Pete McCracken,
Enrique Mosqueda**
Art Director/Designers:
**Niko Courtelis,
Enrique Mosqueda**
Photographer:
Dan Forbes
Client: *IDEA*
magazine (Japan)
Country: **USA**
Year: **2000**

These images were created for the Japanese design magazine *IDEA* for a special issue entitled "Made in America." The inherent health risks in consuming fast food, America's most visible and influential export, is clearly communicated in these simple yet powerful images.

SUPERSIZE

Title: **GMO Good Food**
Format: **Brochure**
Art Director/Designer:
Jarek Bujny
Client: **No client**
Country: **Poland**
Year: **2004**

They don't call genetically
modified food
"Frankenfood" for nothing!
The hairs sprouting out
of this otherwise lovely
looking lemon creates a
repulsive image that warns
of the unknown dangers we
face when playing with
Mother Nature.

genetically modified organism **GOOD FOOD**

Title: **Got Mad Cow?**
Format: **Poster**
Art Director/Designer:
Sharon DiGiacinto
Client: **No client**
Country: **USA**
Year: **2004**

This poster, parodying the
very popular "Got Milk"
campaign and a popular
childhood rhyme, points
out the ironic link between
feeding cows (which are
herbivores) ground-up
body parts of animals and
the creation of mad cow
disease. In 2003, more than
36,800,000 cows were
slaughtered, yet only 20,453
were tested. This frightening
ratio indicates a significant
disregard for public safety
and the care of animals.

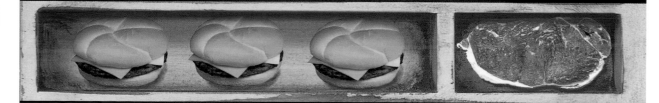

Greasy grimy mammal guts, mutilated mutton meat, disconnected ruminate feet. French fried sheep's eyes rolling down a muddy street, ready to serve to a herbivorous cow. Greasy grimy mammal guts, mutilated mutton meat, disconnected ruminate feet. French fried sheep's eyes rolling down a muddy street, ready to serve to a herbivorous cow

GOT MAD COW?

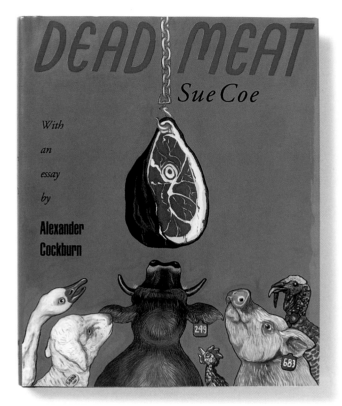

Title: *Dead Meat*
Format: **Book**
Designer/Illustrator:
Sue Coe
Client: **Four Walls
Eight Windows**
Country: **USA**
Year: **1995**

Sue Coe, fine artist,
illustrator, and activist
whose work appears on
street corners as well as at
the Metropolitan Museum
of Art, is a dedicated
animal rights advocate. She
found a way to get herself
inside slaughterhouses in
America to create these
powerful images
documenting the cruelty
and abuse animals
experience in factory
farming.

WHEEL OF FORTUNE
(AT LEFT) UP IN SMOKE

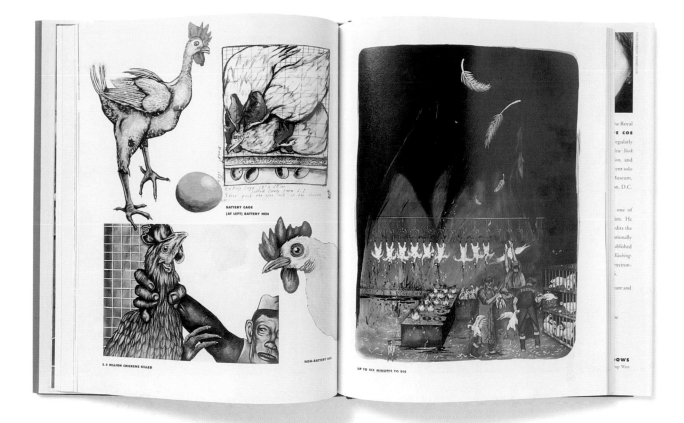

BATTERY CAGE
(AT LEFT) BATTERY HEN

5.5 BILLION CHICKENS KILLED

NON-BATTERY HEN

UP TO SIX MINUTES TO DIE

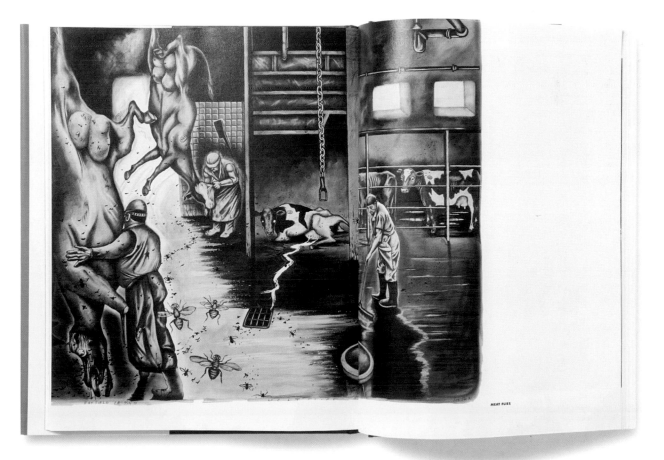

MEAT FLIES

END FACTORY FARMING   DON'T EAT MEAT   1.888.FARM.USA
FARMUSA.ORG

Title: **Dinner**
Format: **Poster series**
Art Director/Designer:
Sandra Scher
Client: **FARM**
Country: **USA**
Year: **2003**

The harsh images of factory
farming are difficult to
bear. The animal rights
organization FARM
wanted to convince people
not to eat meat by
illustrating the cruel
realities of factory farming
with images of dead
animals taking the place of
a dinner plate. The
silverware is arranged in a
place setting to amplify the
consequences of one's
seemingly inconsequential
choice.

END FACTORY FARMING   DON'T EAT MEAT   1.888.FARM.USA
FARMUSA.ORG

Title: **What's Fer Dinner?**
Format: **Cards**
Art Director/Designer:
Kevin Grady
Client: **No client**
Country: **USA**
Year: **2001**

A set of twelve cards,
juxtaposing photographs
taken in a slaughterhouse
with homey, old-fashioned
recipes, provides an
unnerving and powerful
message protesting factory
farming.

Title: **Life**
Format: **Billboard**
Art Director/Designer:
Stanislav Sharp
Photographer:
Vukašin Nedeljković
Client: **No client**
Country: **Serbia and
Montenegro**
Year: **2002**

This billboard campaign
promoting a vegetarian
lifestyle was designed with
a double meaning in mind.
The disturbing image
of chicken heads shown
much larger than life
also reminds viewers to
'preserve life," theirs, and
the lives of other humans.

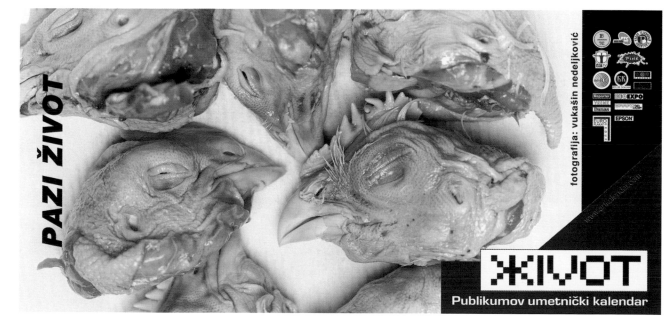

Title: **Death**
Format: **T-shirt**
Art Director/Designer:
Tyler Galloway
Client: **No client**
Country: **USA**
Year: **1998**

The poetic discovery of
the word "eat" within the
word "death" creates the
opportunity to remind
consumers that the
pleasures of one species
require the blood of
another.

Who died for your
dyed fur?

peta2.com

Fake color doesn't mean
fake fur.

peta2.com

Title: **Dyed Fur**
Format: **Print ad**
Art Director/Designer:
Sandra Scher
Client: **PETA**
Country: **USA**
Year: **2004**

The animal activist group
PETA, which introduced a
series of aggressive anti-fur
ads in the 1980s, sponsored
this campaign to alert people to the fact that fur now
comes in bright colors,
because the fur industry
has been dying fur in the
hopes that young women
will mistake it for faux.

Take him from his mom
on the first day of his life.

Keep him in a tiny cage for
the rest of it.

PeTA

If it isn't alright to treat a foal this way, how can it be acceptable treatment for
a calf? When you buy beef and veal from most grocery stores and restaurants,
you support daily animal abuse on factory farms. It just doesn't make sense to
care for some animals and torture others.

Boycott factory farms. www.GoVeg.com

Lock her in a 2 foot wide crate.
Shock her with electric prods.

PeTA

If it isn't alright to treat a dog this way, how can it be acceptable treatment for
a pig? When you buy pork and bacon from most grocery stores and restaurants,
you support daily animal abuse on factory farms. It just doesn't make sense to
care for some animals and torture others.

Boycott factory farms. www.GoVeg.com

Title: **Equal Treatment**
Format: **Ad campaign**
Art Director/Designer:
Sandra Scher
Client: **PETA**
Country: **USA**
Year: **2003**

This ad campaign
highlights the hypocrisy
inherent in being an animal
lover while eating meat. It
raises the question of why
people who would go out of
their way to keep a pet
would turn a blind eye to
the suffering of animals on
factory farms.

Cut off her beak without anesthesia.

Put her in a tiny dark cage so full of
excrement her eyes burn.

PeTA

If it isn't alright to treat a parrot this way, how can it be acceptable treatment
for a chicken? When you buy poultry and eggs from most grocery stores and
restaurants, you support daily animal abuse on factory farms. It just doesn't
make sense to care for some animals and torture others.

Boycott factory farms. www.GoVeg.com

first things first

A manifesto

We, the undersigned, are graphic designers, photographers and students who have been brought up in a world in which the techniques and apparatus of advertising have persistently been presented to us as the most lucrative, effective and desirable means of using our talents. We have been bombarded with publications devoted to this belief, applauding the work of those who have flogged their skill and imagination to sell such things as:

cat food, stomach powders, detergent, hair restorer, striped toothpaste, aftershave lotion, beforeshave lotion, slimming diets, fattening diets, deodorants, fizzy water, cigarettes, roll-ons, pull-ons and slip-ons.

By far the greatest time and effort of those working in the advertising industry are wasted on these trivial purposes, which contribute little or nothing to our national prosperity.

In common with an increasing number of the general public, we have reached a saturation point at which the high pitched scream of consumer selling is no more than sheer noise. We think that there are other things more worth using our skill and experience on. There are signs for streets and buildings, books and periodicals, catalogues, instructional manuals, industrial photography, educational aids, films, television features, scientific and industrial publications and all the other media through which we promote our trade, our education, our culture and our greater awareness of the world.

We do not advocate the abolition of high pressure consumer advertising: this is not feasible. Nor do we want to take any of the fun out of life. But we are proposing a reversal of priorities in favour of the more useful and more lasting forms of communication. We hope that our society will tire of gimmick merchants, status salesmen and hidden persuaders, and that the prior call on our skills will be for worthwhile purposes. With this in mind, we propose to share our experience and opinions, and to make them available to colleagues, students and others who may be interested.

Edward Wright
Geoffrey White
William Slack
Caroline Rawlence
Ian McLaren
Sam Lambert
Ivor Kamlish
Gerald Jones
Bernard Higton
Brian Grimbly
John Garner
Ken Garland
Anthony Froshaug
Robin Fior
Germano Facetti
Ivan Dodd
Harriet Crowder
Anthony Clift
Gerry Cinamon
Robert Chapman
Ray Carpenter
Ken Briggs

Published by Ken Garland.
Printed by Goodwin Press Ltd. London N4

Title: **First Things First**
Format: **Leaflet**
Art Director/Designer:
Ken Garland
Client: **No client**
Country: **UK**
Year: **1964**

This manifesto organized by Ken Garland brought groups of design professionals together to express their concerns about the direction society was going and raised the question of whether designers can act in concert to improve social conditions. It resonated within the design community at the time and the issues it raised are still vital today.

NAME:	Wiseman Ndlovu*
AGE:	Late 20's
ADDRESS:	Homeless (Berea Area - Durban)
MARITAL STATUS	Unmarried - Children (Whereabouts Unknown)
EDUCATION:	Grade 8 (Not Completed)
OCCUPATION:	Currently Unemployed - Part time Car Guard
INCOME 2001-2002:	Tips (Approx. $360)
PERSONAL WEALTH:	Clothing and Personal items - Sports Bag - 2 x Blankets
GENERAL HEALTH:	HIV+ - Persistent Cough - Underweight
PERSONAL DETAILS:	Unfailingly Polite, Trustworthy and Friendly Generally Well Groomed Some in the Area like Wiseman around - but many feel the "Homeless" are a nuisance)
LAST MEAL:	Half Loaf White Bread - 4 Slices Polony Small Portion of Steers Fries 250ml Milk - Half Tin Coke (Donated) 2 Cigarettes (Donated)

NAME:	Gary Winnick*
AGE:	Early 50's
ADDRESS:	Beverly Hills Los Angeles
MARITAL STATUS	Married - Children
EDUCATION:	College Graduate
OCCUPATION:	Chairman Global Crossing (Bankrupt_Under Investigation)
INCOME 1998-2002:	Salary_Stock_Consulting_Aircraft Ownership $750.5m
PERSONAL WEALTH:	Substantial (Though Significantly Reduced)
GENERAL HEALTH:	Good - Overweight
PERSONAL DETAILS:	With the help of his bankers, Gary Winnick treated Global Crossing as his personal cash cow - until the company went bankrupt On a whim over lunch - bought Global Crossing co-chairman a Rolls Royce - and the CEO an Aston Martin
LAST MEAL:	Pan Asian Seared Mahi-Mahi - Small Side Salad Crème Brulée 2 Glasses Napa Valley Chardonay -250ml Mineral Water

© GARTH WALKER
THE WORLD WE LIVE IN . GREED IS GOOD . PART 1
SPOT THE DIFFERENCE #17

* Based on research

* Based on research_Financial Info: FORTUNE June 24 2002

Title: **Shit Piece
(Spot the difference)**
Format: **Magazine spread**
Art Director/Designer:
Garth Walker
Client: *Design
Indaba* magazine
Country: **South Africa**
Year: **2002**

This unpublished piece was commissioned by *Design Indaba*. It was created after the Enron and Worldcom scandals and comments on the outrageous corporate business greed in today's society. The piece points out that when humans are examined at a very basic level, it is clear that we are all equal and there is no difference between the rich and the poor.

Title: **Arm &**
Hammer Logo
Format: **Logo**
Art Director/Designer:
Dejan Krsić
Client: **What, how &**
for whom/WHW
Country: **Croatia**
Year: **2003**

For this logo and signage
for the independent
curators interested in
socially conscious
contemporary art, WHW–
what, how and for whom,
the Arm & Hammer logo
has been re-imagined by
replacing the company
name with the famous
Fluxus slogan, "Art is not a
mirror, it is a hammer!"
The Zagreb designers did
not realize at the time that
the owner of the American
baking soda company, Arm
& Hammer, had a cozy
relationtionship with the
Soviet Union.

Title: **Globalization**
Format: **Sticker**
and poster
Art Director/Designers:
Dejan Krsić,
Dejan Dragosavac Rutta
Client: **IPEG**
(Initiative Against
Economy Globalization)
Country: **Croatia**
Year: **2000**

This anti-globalization
sticker, which reads
"For Globalization of
Freedom and not Corporate
Power," was created
for anti-globalization
demonstrations held in
Zagreb, Croatia at the time
of an international meeting
of economic superpowers
organized by an ad hoc
coalition of various
non-governmental
organizations.

LOS CAMPESINOS DEL MUNDO
APLASTARAN LA GLOBALIZACION

FARM WORKERS OF THE WORLD, UNITE! SMASH THE WTO! 세계의 노동자는 WTO를 탄압한다.

Title: **Hermano Kyang Hae Lee**
Format: **Poster**
Art Director/Designer: **Favianna Rodriguez**
Client: **No client**
Country: **USA**
Year: **2003**

This poster, produced one month after a 50-year-old South Korean farmer died of stab wounds to the chest that were self-inflicted as a protest of WTO policies, calls on farmers to unite against globalization and WTO policies that hurt farmers in third-world countries.

Title: **That's Entertainment!**
Format: **Poster**
Art Director/Designer:
Ward Sutton
Client: **No client**
Country: **USA**
Year: **2003**

The collaboration of news and entertainment produces soldiers as beholden to commercial endorsements as any professional athlete.

Title: **Corporate American Flag**
Format: **Magazine cover**
Art Director/Designer:
Shi-Zhe Yung
Client: *Adbusters*
Country: **Canada**
Year: **2003**

The corporate American flag, with logos in place of stars, has been embraced by Americans who want to declare independence from corporate rule. The image has been re-created into an actual flag used in protests and displayed in communities across the United States and around the world.

Title: **Lucky Strike**
Format: **Poster**
Art Director/Designers:
**Agnieszka Dellfina,
Thomas Dellert-Dellacroix**
Client: **No client**
Country: **France**
Year: **1983**

The central image in this collaged poster is a 1965 cover of *LIFE* magazine depicting a blindfolded and gagged Viet Cong man. The crude implementation of commercial products and the words "war is good business" gives it a certain strength that might not have been present with a more professional execution.

Title: **Happy Meal:
Gypsies, Tramps
and Thieves Mark III**
Format: **Poster**
Art Director/Designer:
Damion Steele
Client: **No client**
Country: **USA**
Year: **2002**

This homage to Da Vinci's *Last Supper* features the McDonalds characters, Hitler, the Bush Administration, Uncle Sam, and a variety of comic characters in a "happy meal," to demonstrate that "fundamentalist zealots and corporations rule our land."

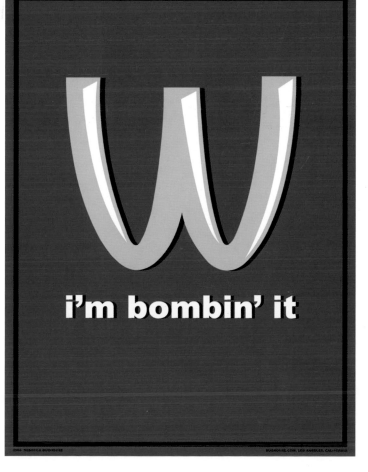

Title: **McDubya**
Format: **Poster**
Art Director/Designer:
Rebecca Bughouse
Client: **No client**
Country: **USA**
Year: **2004**

By flipping one of the most recognizable trademarks in the world, this designer relates George "Dubya" Bush's tactics in promoting his wars to McDonald's relentless marketing to sell its burgers. McDonald's tagline "I'm lovin' it" has been changed to "I'm bombin' it," posing the question: Are consumers willing to buy a war if it is marketed as ambitiously as our manufactured goods?

Title: **Weapons of Mass Destruction**
Format: **Postcard**
Art Director/Designer:
Chaz Maviyane-Davies
Client: **No client**
Country: **USA**
Year: **2004**

The designer ponders, "What are the products of globalization—the silent war?" Often the most pervasive and damaging can seem to be the most innocuous. This postcard is from a series of four entitled "The Language of War."

Title: **Coca-Colonization**
Format: **Poster**
Art Director/Designer:
Chaz Maviyane-Davies
Client: **No client**
Country: **USA**
Year: **2000**

This work illuminating corporate global branding in third-world countries was run in *Adbusters* magazine.

Title: **No to the War**
Format: **Poster and T-shirt**
Art Director/Designer:
Andrés Mario Ramírez Cuevas
Client: **Multiforo Alicia**
Country: **Mexico**
Year: **2003**

Although this image was created to oppose the war in Iraq, it also refers to a larger war between indigenous cultures and the global reach of American corporations, symbolized by Coca-Cola's branding elements, as they supersede the values and economies of the regions they enter.

Title: **Act Against Globalization**
Format: **Poster**
Art Director/Designer: **Richardt Strydom**
Client: **No client**
Country: **South Africa**
Year: **Unknown**

This simple yet powerful image urges viewers to "Employ Molotov" in the fight against globalization. In 1941, the Red Army suffered from "ammo starvation" so petrol bombs were employed to use against tanks. These "bombs," made from fuel and empty glass bottles, were quickly dubbed "Molotov Cocktails." Molotov, during the war years, was Stalin's leading lieutenant, Politburo member, GKO (State Defense Committee) and Sovnarkom vice-chairman.

Title: **United Colors of Netanyahu**
Format: **Poster**
Art Director/Designer: **David Tartakover**
Photographer: **David Krap**
Client: **No client**
Country: **Israel**
Year: **1998**

By playing on racial, ethnic, and religious stereotypes, the fashion company Benetton often used its United Colors campaign to create provocative ads loaded with social commentary. Created during his tenure as Israel's Prime Minister, this poster contrasts the image of Benjamin Netanyahu as a family man with the security requirements that now characterize life in Israel. *(top)*

UNITED COLORS
OF NETANYAHU.

Title: **United Colors of Serbia**
Format: **Magazine cover**
Art Director/Designer: **Vladan Srdić**
Client: *Kvadart* magazine
Country: **Slovenia**
Year: **1999**

This magazine cover parodies the "United Colors of Benetton" campaign to convey that the actual color of Serbia is black—five lost wars in ten years; enormous inflation; one president in prison, the other killed; poverty; and isolation clearly make the case. *(bottom left)*

UNITED COLORS
OF SERBIA

UNITED COLORS
OF HUNG(A)RY 2000.

Title: **United Colors of Hung(a)ry 2000**
Format: **Poster**
Art Director/Designer: **Péter Pócs**
Client: **No client**
Country: **Hungary**
Year: **2000**

This "Thesis-Synthesis" poster illustrates the transformation of the Hungarian Communist Party symbol into the symbol of its successor, the Hungarian Socialist Party. *(bottom right)*

Title: **Citibank**
Format: **Poster series**
Art Director/Designer:
Copper Greene
Client: **No client**
Country: **USA**
Year: **Unknown**

Designed to catch viewers
off-guard, this parody of
the widely recognizable
Citibank campaign that
prompts cardholders to
"Live Richly" asks tougher
questions and proposes
bleaker answers than its
less-political counterpart.

Title: **Plakate-Disney**
Format: **Poster**
Art Directors:
**Lars Harmsen,
Ulrich Weiß, Lutz Wahler,
Michael Lutz**
Designer: **Ulrich Weiß**
Client: **Gruppe 10**
Country: **Germany**
Year: **1994**

This poster is part of a
collection designed by
Gruppe 10 that was sent
to subscribers a few weeks
before the chancellor
election in Germany. The
image suggests that Mickey
Mouse is a symbol of
western cultural
globalization. *(top)*

Title: **Bloody Mickey**
Format: **Poster**
Art Director/Designer:
Qian Qian
Client: **No client**
Country: **USA**
Year: **Unknown**

We are all targets of
consumerism, but in this
depiction of Mickey Mouse,
the artist has reversed that
position. *(bottom left)*

Title: **Boycott campaign**
Format: **Poster**
Art Director/Designers:
Nour Saab, Reem Kotob
Client: **A group
of Lebanese and
international activists**
Country: **Lebanon**
Year: **2002**

These fliers were
distributed to Lebanese
consumers in hopes that
the public would boycott
Nestles and Estee Lauder,
both of whom support
Israel. *(far right; top
& bottom)*

ESTĒE LAUDER
FOR ALL TIME. FOR ISRAEL.

Title: **War Wear Rifle**
Format: **Poster**
Art Director/Designer:
Tomato Košir
Client: **No client**
Country: **Slovenia**
Year: **2000**

Rifle is a trendy Italian jeans company that targets what they call the "cyberpunk generation." Created as an anti-war poster, this simple yet potent imagery contrasts the frivolity of our consumer-driven lifestyle with the horror of war.

Title: *VW Spoof Ad*
Format: **Poster**
Art Director/Designer:
Matt Erceg
Client: **No client**
Country: **USA**
Year: **2001**

This design spoofs ads for the cute Volkswagen everyone loves by reminding the viewer who was responsible for supporting the development of the original "people's car," as they were known when first produced in Germany, by inserting an image of Hitler in his own Volkswagen.

Title: **Hummer**
Format: **Magazine spread**
Art Director/Designer:
Matt Campbell
Client: *BIG* magazine
Country: **USA**
Year: **2004**

These ads attacking SUV ownership were designed by a group called Greedy Gas Guzzlers for *BIG* magazine. The images that were allowed to run were ultimately reduced to thumbnails because Hummer objected to them and would not advertise in the magazine unless they were removed.

Title: **Pay Us to Kill You**
Format: **Poster**
Art Director/Designer:
G. Dan Covert
Client: **California College
of the Arts**
Country: **USA**
Year: **2001**

This artist's grandmother
passed away after a long
battle with emphysema,
which provoked this poster
focusing on how profitable
the tobacco industry
has been while promoting
illness and death.

Title: **Los Gatos California: What Right Do They Take Away Next?**
Format: **T-shirt**
Art Director/Designer: **Unknown**
Client: **Unknown**
Country: **USA**
Year: **Unknown**

This reaction to a nonsmoking ban in bars and restaurants in Los Gatos, California, one of the first municipalities that enforced the ban on smoking, included T-shirts that were given to municipal officers as protest gifts to show their displeasure with this policy.

Title: **Don't Smoke**
Format: **Poster**
Art Director/Designers: **Albino Uršić, Boris Kuk**
Client: **No client**
Country: **Croatia**
Year: **1994**

Nazi images, which immediately get viewers' attention and allude to the idea of gas chambers, suggest that cigarette companies do not care if they kill you.

STOP THE ARROGANCE

Title: **Stop the Arrogance**
Format: **Poster**
Art Director/Designers:
**Nicholas Blechman,
Michael Mabry**
Client: *NOZONE
IX/EMPIRE*
Country: **USA**
Year: **2003**

This poster, entered in an exhibition sponsored by the Hong Kong International Poster Triennial 2004, expresses the frustrations U.S. citizens have with the Bush Administration's lack of environmental policies. The gun-slinging cowboy, "trashing everything in its path" while polluting the air and water, reflects not only the United States government's lack of interest in protecting the environment, but also the arrogance and lack of caring for the general welfare of the rest of the Earth.

Title: **Stop the Plant**
Format: **Poster**
Art Director/Designer:
Woody Pirtle/Pentagram
Client: **Scenic Hudson**
Country: **USA**
Year: **2003**

This poster was a part of a grassroots campaign against the construction of a mammoth cement plant that would emit 20 million pounds of pollutants each year on the east bank of the Hudson in upstate New York. Environmental preservation and concerned citizen groups sponsored the campaign.

Title: **Brainwashing**
Format: **Magazine ad**
Art Director/Designer:
Vladan Srdić
Client: *Mlandia* **magazine**
Country: **Slovenia**
Year: **2003**

This image of a dial on a washing machine, labeled with the major television netwoks in America, protests the manipulation of the American mass media, who brainwash the public to support war and aggression.

BRAINWASHING

Title: Your Death—Our
Business!
Format: **Poster**
Art Director/Designers:
**Agnieszka Dellfina,
Thomas Dellert-Dellacroix**
Client: **No client**
Country: **France**
Year: **2002**

War is good business,
especially for news
organizations.
Sensationalistic news
always attracts viewers
and, thus, advertising
dollars.

Title: **Reality TV**
Format: **Poster**
Art Director/Designer:
Peter Kuper
Client:
AnotherPosterforPeace.org
Country: **USA**
Year: **2002**

This ghostly downloadable image playing off the abundance of reality shows dominating the networks was produced for antiwar marches in NYC before the Iraq War began.

Title: **Breaking News**
Format: **Postcard**
Art Director/Designer:
Ward Sutton
Client: **No client**
Country: **USA**
Year: **2003**

Embedded American journalists were seduced and manipulated into becoming propagandists during the Iraq War, dutifully reporting the toppling of the Saddam Hussein statue in the news media. This postcard served as an invitation/announcement for an event the artist sponsored on the failing of the media.

Title: **Independence**
Format: **Poster**
Art Director/Designer:
Sonja Smith
Client: **No client**
Country: **USA**
Year: **2003**

This personal expression of dissent was created by the artist for posting in the street on 4th of July (Independence Day), 2003, in opposition to corporate control of the media.

Title: **Media Democracy Day**
Format: **Poster and logo**
Art Director/Designer:
Valerie Thai
Client: **Campaign for Press and Broadcast Freedom**
Country: **Canada**
Year: **2002–2003**

The image of a clenched fist as a speech balloon was created for Canada's Media Democracy Day created to protest the dominant mass media system and promote independent media and citizens fighting for their right to news and information, and their basic right to communicate their opinions.

Title: **Hope**
Format: **Poster**
Art Director/Designer:
Charlie Ross
Client: **No client**
Country: **USA**
Year: **1999**

This poster encourages the public to transcend the overwhelming presence of tabloid media and its obsession with violence and scandal. The artist comments, "To believe you can move beyond your mistakes, to me, defines hope."

Title: **As Seen on TV**
Format: **Poster**
Art Director/Designer:
Jeff Louviere
Client: **The American™ Dream**
Country: **USA**
Year: **2000**

The image is provocative, but the statistic noting that, by the age of 18, American children will have witnessed 16,000 murders on television is even more so.

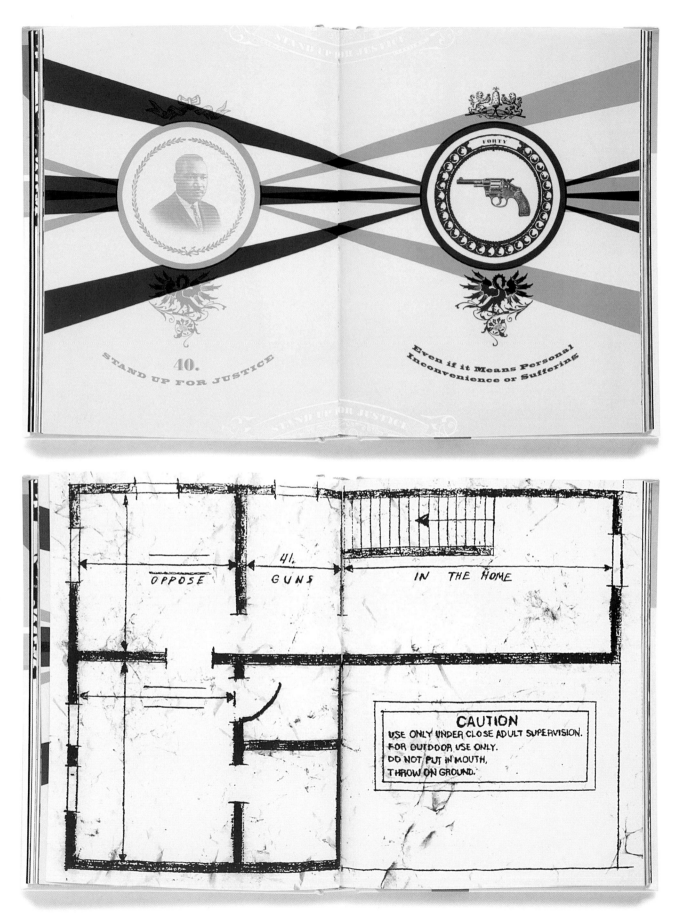

Title: *Peace: 100 Ideas*
Format: **Book**
Art Director/Designers:
**Joshua Chen,
Max Spector,
Jennifer Tolo**
Client: **Chen Design
Associates**
Country: **USA**
Year: **2004**

Printed on 100%
post-consumer, recycled
stock, this booklet
imaginatively illustrates
100 ideas for a more
peaceful world such as,
"stand up for justice even
if it means personal
inconvenience or
suffering."

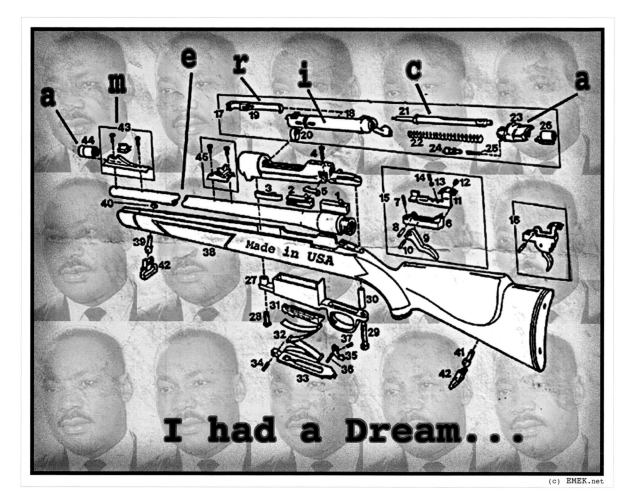

(c) EMEK.net

Title: **I Had a Dream**
Format: **Poster**
Art Director/Designer:
Emek
Client: **No client**
Country: **USA**
Year: **1999**

Headshots of assassinated American civil rights leader Martin Luther King, Jr. form the background for this image, illustrating a brief history of American gun violence.

Title: **Republican Contract on America**
Format: **Poster**
Art Director/Designer:
Mark Fox
Client: **No client**
Country: **USA**
Year: **1995**

This image was created in response to Newt Gingrich's widely publicized, "Contract with America." Along with a quote by Nazi Hermann Goering, powerful figures of the Republican Party are depicted as all the working parts of a gun, minus the sight, which the designer purposely omitted. The headline "Republican Contract on America" changes the word "with" to "on," eluding to the mafia's terminology for killing someone.

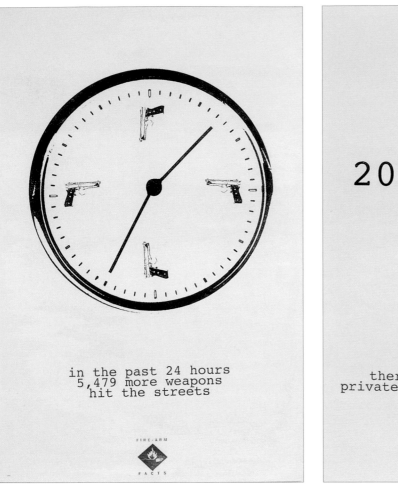

in the past 24 hours
5,479 more weapons
hit the streets

FIRE-ARM
FACTS

200000,000

there are over 200 million
privately held guns in the u.s.a.

FIRE-ARM
FACTS

Title: **Fire Arms Facts**
Format: **Poster**
Art Director/Designers:
**Kerry Stratford,
Herb Stratford**
Client: **No client**
Country: **USA**
Year: **1994**

This guerilla poster
campaign was created to
educate people about
firearm dangers. The state
of Arizona grants concealed
weapon permits to private
citizens. The artist hoped
putting posters containing
the plain facts about guns
on display in downtown
Tucson would provoke
discussions about the
impact of guns on society.

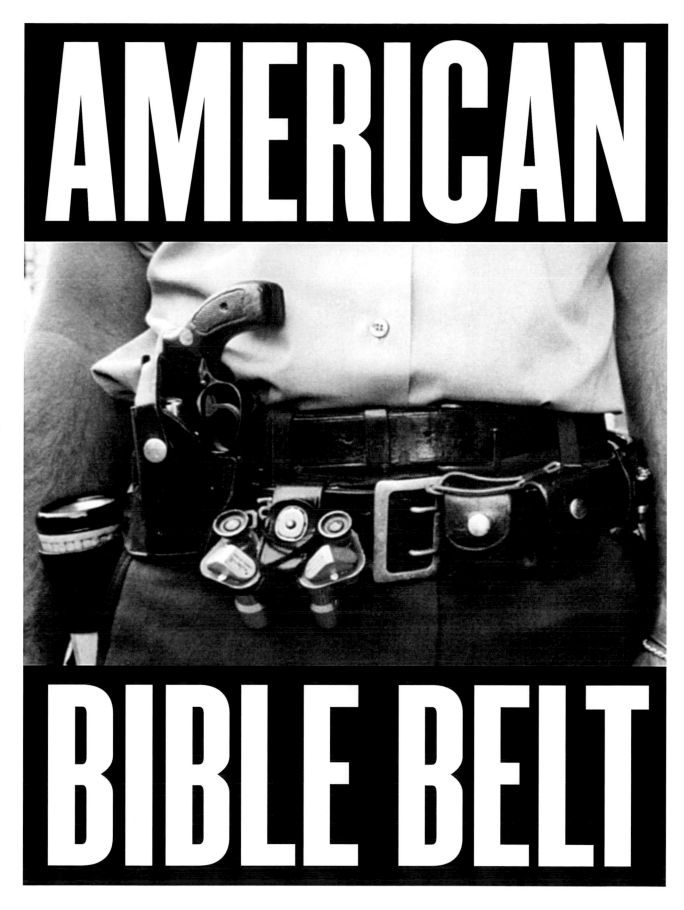

Title: **American Bible Belt**
Format: **Poster**
Art Director/Designer:
John Yates
Client: **Stealworks**
Country: **USA**
Year: **1995**

This poster is a tough comment on the relationship between fundamentalism and violence in the United States.

Title: **Curb Your God**
Format: **T-shirt**
Art Director/Designer:
Daniel Young
Client: **No client**
Country: **USA**
Year: **2004**

This T-shirt illustrates
the designer's personal
objection to the worldwide
increase in violence
and intolerance based on
so-called divine
instructions.

Title: **Beware of God**
Format: **Metal sign**
Art Director/Designer:
Mark Fox
Client: **No client**
Country: **USA**
Year: **1992**

This piece parodies a
common sign used at the
entrance to one's home:
"Beware of Dog." The artist
comments that he created
it "as a public service
announcement."

Title: **Pray Nike**
Format: **Video**
Art Director/Designers:
**Javier Freeman,
Gabriel Freeman**
Client: **Un Mundo Feliz/A
Happy World Production**
Country: **Spain**
Year: **2003**

Created for an online video exhibition, familiar religious symbols are transformed into the omnipresent Nike swoosh logo, a potent symbol that represents a time when consumerism has become a new religion. *(top)*

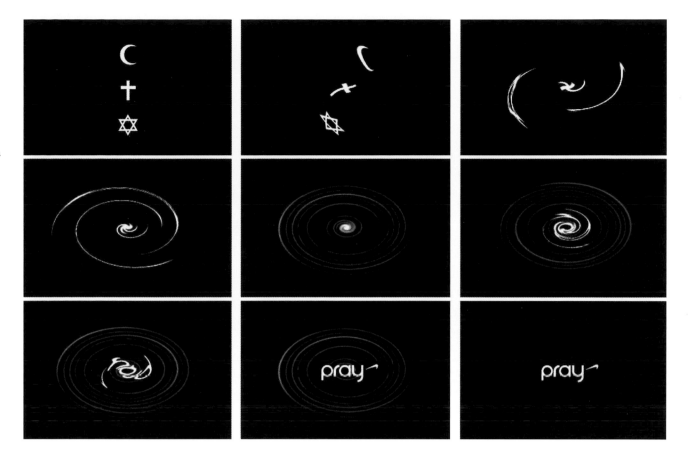

Title: **Faith**
Format: **Unknown**
Art Director/Designer:
Grzegorz Hańderek
Client: **Unknown**
Country: **Poland**
Year: **2001**

This designer proposes that there is not only one right belief, but that there are many routes one can follow in the name of faith. *(bottom left)*

Title: **Jihad**
Format: **Sticker
and stamps**
Art Director/Designer:
Garland Kirkpatrick
Client: **No client**
Country: **USA**
Year: **2001**

Stickers and stamps were made to point out the irony of Bush's fundamentalist cowboy crusade against terrorism. They were used during the antiwar rallies throughout Los Angeles after September 2001. "Jihad!" sounds like "Yee Haw!" something shouted by a cowboy on a bucking bronco. *(bottom right)*

faith

JiHAD

KRUISPAD

Title: **Crossroads**
Format: **Poster**
Art Director/Designer:
Neels de Coning
Client:
Constantia Dr Church
Country: **South Africa**
Year: **2001**

The Dutch Reformed
Church in Cape Town
attempted to transform a
white Afrikaans speaking
church into a multiracial
congregation; "Kruispad"
means crossroads. The
compass underpins a crown
of thorns to represent
Christ's compassion and
the desire to bring about
change.

Title: *Coloring Book:*
A Contemporary Art
Project
Format: **Coloring book**
Art Director/Designers:
Sener Ozmen,
Ahmet Ogut
Client: **Cetinje Biennial V**
Country: **Turkey**
Year: **2004**

The artists created this
coloring book parody or
"Turkish ghost history,"
based on their own
childhood experiences
of schizoid images and
historical "reality." The
work does not portray any
particular ethnic group or
nation, rather it illustrates
the realities of the homes
of a certain part of the
population and "the
conditions under which the
visual intelligence of our
children develop."

Title: **Dźihad**
Format: **Poster**
Art Director/Designer:
Ewa Wlostowska
Client: **No client**
Country: **Poland**
Year: **2002**

Magritte's everyday man
here serves to represent the
idea of an ordinary
European being connected
to Jihad. The figure is a
secret fighter ready to
assume the green color of
Jihad and start fighting for
the cause at a moment's
notice.

Title: **Impuls**
Format: **Poster**
Art Director/Designer:
Ewa Wlostowska
Client: **No client**
Country: **Poland**
Year: **2002**

This poster utilizes the
simplicity of a symbol to
suggest a broader message
about the transmission of
ideas and information. This
artist's suggestion is that to
be recognized one must
make waves or send
impulses throughout the
world. The symbol used
here is one that has come
to represent Islam, the
crescent and the star.

Title: **Hasta La Victoria Siempre (Until Victory Always)**
Format: **Poster**
Art Director/Designer: **Anatoliy Omelchenko**
Client: **No client**
Country: **USA**
Year: **2004**

One man's terrorist is another man's freedom fighter. The designer makes this point in this poster by placing the famous image of Ernesto "Che" Guevara against a green background symbolizing the Muslim religion and adding a crescent moon to the pre-existing star on his beret to symbolize Islam.

Title: **Medals
of Dishonour**
Format: **Postcard**
Art Director/Designer:
Chaz Maviyane-Davies
Client: **No client**
Country: **USA**
Year: **2002**

This piece was created in
response to a statement
made by defense forces
commander General Vitalis
Zvinavashe, the day that
President Robert Mugabe
kicked off his campaign, in
which he noted that he and
the security organizations
would not support anyone
with a "different agenda
that threatens the
very existence of our
sovereignty, our country,
and our people."

Title: **DRC/Impunity/**
Fear Is the Best Weapon
Format: **Postcards**
Art Director/Designer:
Chaz Maviyane-Davies
Client: **No client**
Country: **USA**
Year: **2002**

This postcard telling viewers "Do not be intimidated. Use your vote and be counted. Our fear is their best weapon." is a response to the redeployment of the 5th Brigade into Matebeleland, which added a psychological twist to the continued intimidation campaign in Zimbabwe.

The designer comments, "Robert Mugabe sent our troops to die in a war in the Democratic Republic of Congo. It had nothing to do with the interest of the citizens of Zimbabwe but with his personal greed." (*opposite bottom left*)

"T-shirts are a life-and-death matter in Zimbabwe. Wear an opposition T-shirt and you become a walking target. The ruling party's (ZANU) T-shirt, on the other hand, allows the wearer immunity from the authorities." This design converts the A to the anarchist symbol to reflect the current reality. (*opposite bottom right*)

Title: **Rastros Unbanos Archivo Graffitero**
Format: **Street art- Combined stencil and graffiti**
Art Director/Designer: **Anonymous**
Photos: **Emilio Petersen's Rastros Urbanos– Archivo Graffitero**
Client: **No client**
Country: **Argentina**
Year: **2003**

This collection of stenciled graffiti printed on Buenos Aires city walls is part of a project examining street graffiti (www.elportalde-mexico.com). The material, gathered from mid-2003 to the present day, includes approximately 1,600 images and reveals that the medium is often used to voice political discontent.

This stencil points out the ironic and opportune capture of Saddam Hussein just before Christmas in 2003. *(top left)*

One can only assume the artist's intent with this stencil of George W. Bush as Mickey Mouse. *(top right)*

An American female is shown bowling with a bomb, symbolizing America's abuse of force in its attempts to solve international conflicts. *(bottom left)*

An anarchist's redesign of Milton Glaser's iconic logotype replaces the heart with a bomb. *(bottom right)*

This stencil combines Roberto Santucho, a Trotskyist leader of the PRT and ERP political movements in the 1970s, Ernesto Che Guevara, and the word "Exocet," which was the missile that was used to sink several English ships during the Malvinas (Falklands) war in 1982. (*top*)

Argentina Arde (Argentina Burns), a group of young artist activists who came together during the 2001 social conflicts, promotes itself with this two-color stencil of its logo. (*bottom left*)

The Ford Falcon was the government vehicle of choice for kidnapping citizens and the year of the coup d' etat is noted on the license plate. Many people believe the present exhortation kidnappings are being performed by mass-murderers still on the police force in Argentina. (*bottom right*)

Title: **No a la militarizacion en America Latina**
Format: **Street art—stencil**
Art Director/Designer: **Anonymous**
Photos: **Emilio Petersen's Rastros Urbanos— Archivo Graffitero**
Client: **No client**
Country: **Argentina**
Year: **2004**

This stencil signifies a clear resistance to the militarization of Latin America.

Title: **Mass Murderers Live Here**
Format: **Street art—poster and two-color stencil**
Art Director/Designer: **Anonymous**
Photos: **Emilio Petersen's Rastros Urbanos— Archivo Graffitero**
Client: **No client**
Country: **Argentina**
Year: **2003**

The redesigned world cup logo of 1978 shows the date, and the map reveals the locations of the clandestine detention centers and the torturer's addresses from that time.

Title: **Se cayo el sistema
(The system falls)**
Format:
Street art—stencil
Art Director/Designer:
**BsAsTCL (Buenos Aires
Stencil Group)**
Photos: **Emilio Petersen's
Rastros Urbanos—
Archivo Graffitero**
Client: **No client**
Country: **Argentina**
Year: **2004**

The sinking of the
Titanic makes an
effective background for
the pun made from the
revolutionary slogan of the
1960s and 70s: "Hay que
destruir el systema
(We must destroy the
capitalist system)," and
the contemporary
computer-speak, "The
system collapsed."

DIGNIDAD REBELDE, IDENTIDAD NACIONAL
Por el Reconocimiento Constitucional de los Acuerdos de San Andrés
México 2001

Title: **Rebel Dignity, National Identity**
Format: **Poster**
Art Director/Designer: **Leonel Sagahón**
Client: **La Corriente Eléctrica**
Country: **Mexico**
Year: **2001**

Fingerprints represent identity. This artist removed the center of a fingerprint to emphasize two key aspects of the Mexican Zapatista movement. The first is the lost identity of Mexico's indigenous people. The second is the hidden identity of the rebels symbolized by the formation of a ski mask. Created in 2001 to support the Zapatista march on Mexico City petitioning for constitutional recognition, this poster focuses attention on the complexity of having to hide one's own identity in order to regain it for others. *(top left)*

Title: **We Are the Rebellious Dignity**
Format: **Poster**
Art Director/Designer: **Andrés Mario Ramírez Cuevas**
Client: **FZLN**
Country: **Mexico**
Year: **2004**

This powerful graphic image commemorates the tenth anniversary of the Zapatista uprising, perhaps the most significant event in indigenous Mexico's struggle for freedom and justice since the 1910 Revolution. The combination of the ski mask, the left wing–oriented red tongue, and the words "we are the rebel dignity" conveys the passion behind the Zapatista movement as symbolized by this bold, and undeniably dynamic, composition. *(top right)*

Title: **Day of the Dead**
Format: **Poster**
Art Director/Designer: **Jesus Barraza**
Client: **No client**
Country: **USA**
Year: **2001**

This poster was made for the 2001 Day of the Dead celebration in San Francisco. The artist chose to dedicate it to all the people who have fallen during the Zapatista struggle in Chiapas, Mexico. *(bottom)*

Title: **Queen of Mexico and the Empress of America**
Format: **Poster**
Art Director/Designer: **David Rojas**
Client: **No client**
Country: **Mexico**
Year: **1994**

This poster was designed for the first anniversary of the left-wing, religious Zapatista uprising in Chiapas, Mexico. The "ski" mask (which the Zapatistas are known to wear to protect their identity and avoid being targeted by the government) symbolizes the revolution and the desperate state of mind of a very divided, punished, and quite forgotten community inside Mexico. The Virgin of Guadalupe symbolizes unity, solidarity, hope, and "mexicanidad," the unifying and healing power of religion.

REINA DE MÉXICO Y EMPERATRIZ DE AMERICA

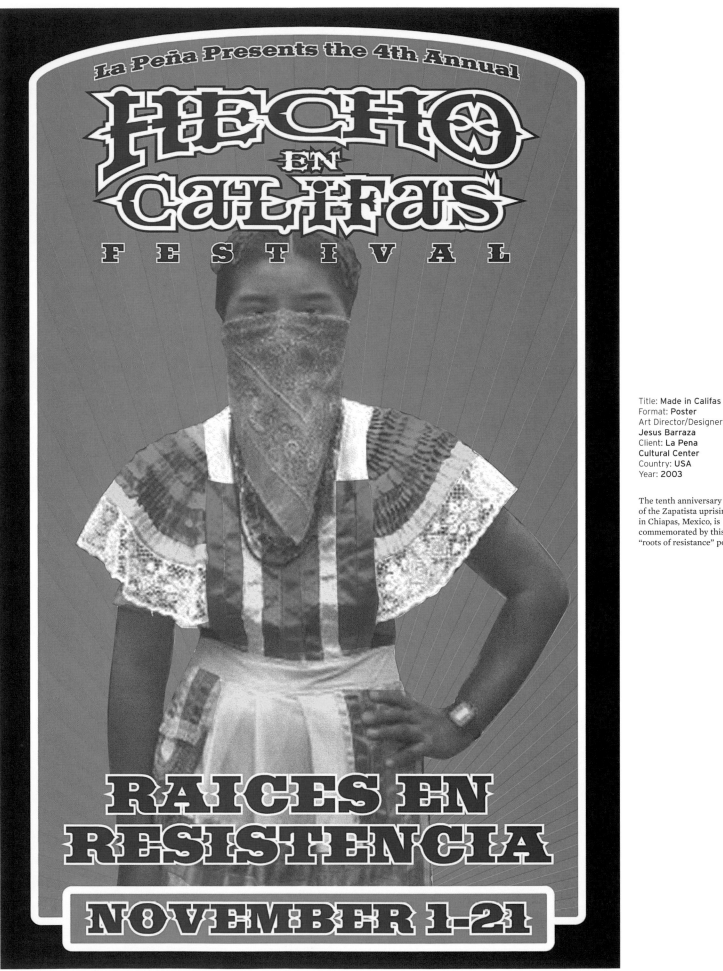

Title: **Made in Califas**
Format: **Poster**
Art Director/Designer:
Jesus Barraza
Client: **La Pena
Cultural Center**
Country: **USA**
Year: **2003**

The tenth anniversary
of the Zapatista uprising
in Chiapas, Mexico, is
commemorated by this
"roots of resistance" poster.

Title: **We Shall Overcome**
Format: **Poster**
Art Director/Designer:
Leonel Sagahón
Client: **1968–1998 Project**
Country: **Mexico**
Year: **1998**

The 1968 Mexican student movement protesting the government's decision to invest in hosting the Olympic Games when the country was suffering extreme poverty celebrated its thirtieth anniversary with this poster. The design symbolically depicts the events of that day in which the army gunned down hundreds of people in Tlatelolco Square just before the beginning of the Games. Mexican religious imagery tends to be quite visceral, hence the more realistic version of a heart rather than a more stylistic one.

Title: **The Missing Ones**
Format: **Poster**
Art Director/Designer:
Leonel Sagahón
Client: **No client**
Country: **Mexico**
Year: **2004**

More than 500 people disappeared after detainment by Mexican authorities. This poster asks, "Where are they? The forced disappearance of people is a crime that remains unpunished in our country."

¿DÓNDE ESTÁN?

DES PAREC DOS

EN MÉXICO MÁS DE 500 PERSONAS HAN DESAPARECIDO DESPUÉS DE HABER SIDO DETENIDAS POR LAS AUTORIDADES. LA DESAPARICIÓN FORZADA DE PERSONAS, ES UN DELITO CONTRA LA HUMANIDAD QUE EN NUESTRO PAÍS PERMANECE IMPUNE.

TIPOGRAFÍA: EL LENGUAJE VISIBLE

Title: **September 1978: Managua, Nicaragua**
Format: **Poster**
Art Director/Designer: **Fermin Gonzalez**
Client: **Managua, Nicaragua**
Country: **USA**
Year: **Unknown**

September 1978 was a particularly bloody month in the Nicaraguan insurrection. The text on the poster along each bullet hole reads "Your Papa was a good son/Your Papa played the guitar/Your Papa was only 21 years old/Your Papa was a good husband." The insurrectionary war that brought down a fifty-year dictatorship in Nicaragua and put the Sandinistas in power in 1979 took thousands of lives, many of them civilians.

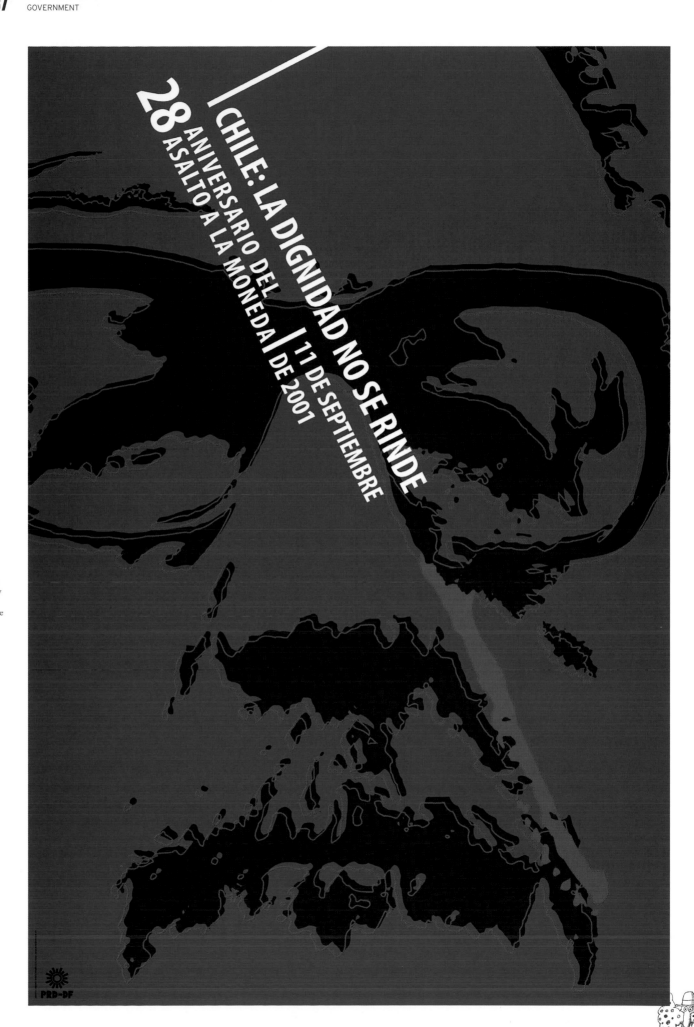

Title: **Chile: Dignity Does Not Surrender**
Format: **Poster**
Art Director/Designer: **Andrés Mario Ramírez Cuevas**
Client: **PRD-DF**
Country: **Mexico**
Year: **2001**

This expressionistic portrait of Salvador Allende, assassinated democratic president of Chile, commemorates the twenty-eighth anniversary of the coup d'etat by the Chilean military, led by the future dictator Augusto Pinochet.

Title: *Violence*
Format: **Poster**
Art Director/Designer:
Pedram Harby
Client: **No client**
Country: **Iran**
Year: **2004**

The shadow cast by a
skewered IKEA doll
(skewering was once a
traditional method of
torture in Iran) shows no
one is safe from the
violence that is inherent in
mankind.

Title: **The Struggle**
Format: **Poster**
Art Director/Designer:
Pedram Harby
Client: **No client**
Country: **Iran**
Year: **2003**

The text on this Iranian
poster reads, "Whatever
the struggle, continue the
climb, it may be only one
step to the summit!" The
oppressed peoples of the
world, despite different
cultures and environments,
have the same hopes and
dreams as echoed by
Martin Luther King, Jr.'s
infamous 1968 speech, "I've
been to the mountaintop."

Title: **In Memoriam Kaveh**
Format: **Poster**
Art Director/Designer:
Majid Abbasi
Client: **No client**
Country: **Iran**
Year: **2003**

This poster commemorates
renowned photojournalist
Kaveh Golestan, who in
2003, after decades of
covering conflicts in the
Middle East, was killed
by a landmine while on
assignment in northern
Iraq. This powerful image
is a detail from one of
Golestan's photographs
taken during 1979 student
uprisings at the University
of Tehran.

کاوه

عکس

انقلاب

مردم

جوان

عکاس

دانشگاه

حکومت نظامی

کردستان

ترکمن صحرا

جنگ

تظاهرات

جایزه ی پولیتزر

دوربین

سربازان مسلح

سانسور

اهواز

آبادان

شلمچه

عراق

ژورنالیست

حقیقت

کودکان

Majid Abbasi 2003

... به یاد کاوه گلستان

افغانستان

رنج

آتش

دود

شیمیایی

بمباران

انسان

چاپ هفتم

سعید حجاریان

جمهوریت؛

افسون زدایی از قدرت

Title: *Republicanism*
Format: **Book cover**
Art Director/Designer:
Bijan Sayfouri
Client: **Tarh-e Now**
Publishers
Country: **Iran**
Year: **Unknown**

This cover for
Republicanism:
Demystification of Power
depicts King Tahmash,
leader of the historic
Iranian dictatorship, being
obscured by democracy,
represented by a voting
box, as a means of
contrasting these two
types of societies.

Title: The Grim Reaper
Format: Newspaper
cartoon
Illustrator: Ali Ferzat
Client: *Al Domari*
newspaper
Country: Syria
Year: Mid-'90s

Because of this and similar cartoons published in Ferzat's newspaper *Al Domari*, the only privately owned newspaper in Syria, the Syrian government newspaper published editorials against Ferzat two days in a row, proclaiming it was shameful to make fun of the Iraqi regime while it boldly stood up against superpower invaders. In addition, hundreds of protesters picketed *Al Domari's* offices.

Title: *Dictators in the Mirror of Medicine*
Format: Book cover
Art Director/Designer:
Bijan Sayfouri
Client:
Agah Publishing House
Country: Iran
Year: Unknown

This cover for the book *Dictators in the Mirror of Medicine: Napoleon, Hitler and Stalin* represents Hitler as a psychopath, the universal symbol of cruel dictatorship across borders. *(bottom left)*

Title: Right to Information
Format: Poster
Art Director/Designer:
Sanjeev Bothra
Client: MKSS—Majdur, Kisan, Shakti, Sangathan
Country: India
Year: 2001

The triangular intersection of politician, police, and bureaucrat illustrates the endemic corruption in India. This poster was commissioned by an Indian nongovernmental agency sponsoring a workshop called, "The Right to Information." The text on the poster notes that the state has been ruled under the shadow of scams and that too much theft has taken place. It asks "Someone speak up, at least open your mouth." *(bottom right)*

Title: **Banners for March**
Format: **Banners**
Art Director/Designer:
Ken Garland
Client: **CND**
Country: **UK**
Year: **1963**

Ken Garland worked with
Peggy Duff to pull together
this groundbreaking protest
in which they provided
various branches of the
campaign for Nuclear
Disarmament with stencils,
black fabric, and specifications
on banner content and
height. Each branch was
asked to stencil their name
on one side of the banner
and a slogan on the reverse,
which involved the
participants in the event on
a more immediate level.
The participants then
surrounded Windsor Castle
in its entirety—a feat no
longer possible in today's
society.

Title: **Puzzle Pieces**
Format: **Illustration, sign**
Art Director/Designer:
Rebecca Migdal
Client: **No client**
Country: **USA**
Year: **2003**

The puzzle showing how
various events link up to
complete a large historical
picture was designed at a
World War III Arts in
Action workshop. The
pieces were later used as a
group of signs during a
massive 2004 peace rally in
New York City.

Title: **Free Trade Area of the Americas**
Format: **Banner**
Art Director/Designer:
Behive Design Collective
Client: **anti-copyright non-profit**
Country: **USA**
Year: **Unknown**

The Free Trade Area of the Americas (FTAA), which has been negotiated in private since 1994, aims to eliminate the remaining "barriers" to the free flow of money, goods, and services across borders in the Western Hemisphere, excluding Cuba, in an attempt to create one huge, integrated web of "open markets." This graphic representation of it illustrates the consequences of this network, and exposes its threat to all forms of life throughout the Americas and is a tool for educating people about the overwhelming effects of a monoculture. *(top)*

Title: **Poder**
Format: **Installation**
Art Director/Designers:
Grupo Calljero Periferia/ Benites, Corda, Doberti, Kuperman, and Zech
Client: **People of Buenos Aires City**
Country: **Argentina**
Year: **2002**

On December 20, 2001, Argentinians went to the streets demanding that banks give back their savings, which had been confiscated to pay Argentina's debt. This ultimately caused the collapse of the government and resulted in twenty-nine deaths. One year later, the urban art group Periferia conjugated the verb "poder" (which means "power" and "can") on a fence erected one year previous to protect the "government's house," the embodiment of corrupt power. *(bottom left)*

Title: **Siamo Uomini o Cavalieri?**
Format: **Poster**
Art Director/Designer:
Andrea Rauch
Client: **CGIL (Italian Syndicate)**
Country: **Italy**
Year: **2002**

Totó, Italy's beloved actor is used here to pose his well-remembered question, "Are we men or foremen?" in reference to allegedly corrupt Italian Prime Minister Berlusconi, who owns and controls most of the media in Italy. In Italian, "foreman" carries negative connotations of one who torments other men. *(bottom right)*

Title: **Move Our Money**
Format: **Various**
Art Director/Designers:
**Stefan Sagmeister,
Hjalti Karlsson**
Client: **Business Leaders
for Sensible Priorities**
Country: **USA**
Year: **1999**

The familiar Crayola colors
and simple designs in
this series of works make
the huge, complex
Pentagon budget figures
comprehensible and
simple. Some of the charts,
designed as enormous
inflatable sculptures,
formed part of a traveling
road show featuring the
Move Our Money mobile.
These displays provided
a little (but hopefully
hard-hitting) information
on a large scale. Other
items such as T-shirts,
statistic cards, and pens
were given away to
spectators during the
traveling show. Ben Cohen,
of Ben & Jerry's ice cream,
formed Business Leaders
for Sensible Priorities,
an initiative to move 15
percent of the Pentagon
budget to education and
health care.

Title: **True Majority**
Format: **Various**
Art Director/Designers:
Stefan Sagmeister,
Matthias Ernstberger
Client: **True Majority**
Country: **USA**
Year: **2002**

This logo was designed for a grassroots education and advocacy group led by Ben Cohen (cofounder of Ben & Jerry's) and comprised of 200 business leaders, CEOs, and military advisers. The group's goals are to pressure the government to adopt long-term policies designed to prevent another 9/11 by dealing with world hunger, reducing dependence on oil, and paying our UN dues. (*top left*)

These pink piggy cars compare and contrast the Pentagon budget (the first pink car in line) to the spending on education (the second pink car) and foreign aid (the third). (*top right*)

These cars, which focus on saving energy, conserving the environment, and reducing our oil dependence, are being driven throughout the United States. The designer notes, "As a base, the hybrid Toyota Prius was used. If all cars on the road in the United States would achieve the same gas mileage as the Prius, no Middle East oil would have to be imported." The goal was to get the cars featured on local TV news channels, thereby forcing newscasters to explain what the campaign was about. (*bottom*)

WE SWIM AGAINST THE TIDE

WITHIN YOUR MAINSTREAM

Title: **Swimming Against the Tide**
Format: **Poster**
Art Director/Designer: **John Yates**
Client: **Stealworks**
Country: **USA**
Year: **Unknown**

In the tradition of John Heartfield's powerful photomontaged *AIZ* magazine covers, this poster juxtaposes a peaceful street scene from the "Golden Fifties" with a diametrically opposed one of urban warfare.

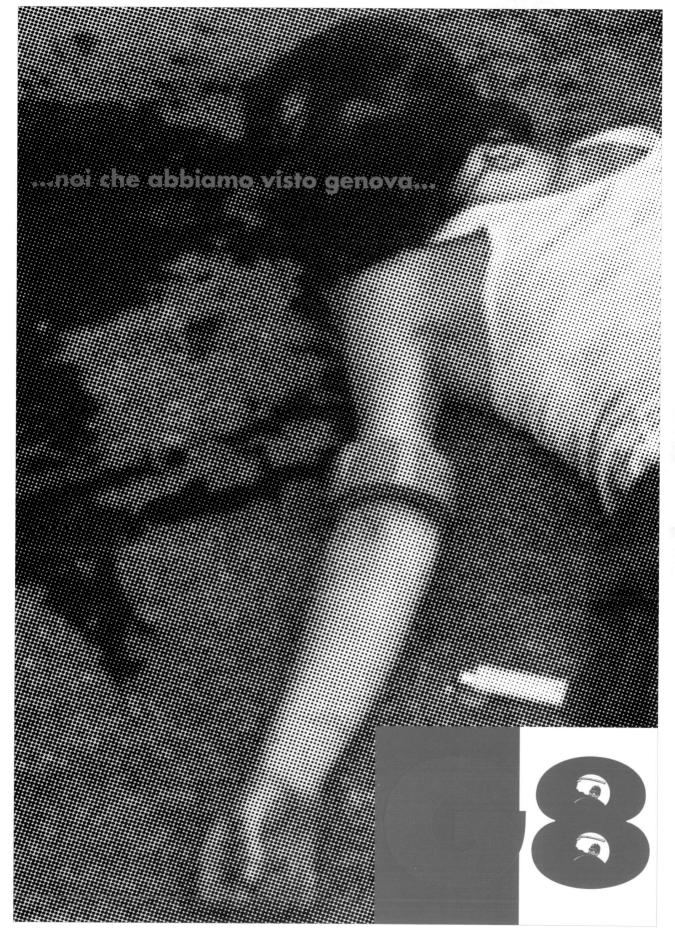

...noi che abbiamo visto genova...

Title: G8
Format: **Poster**
Art Director/Designer:
Andrea Rauch
Client: **ARCI**
Country: **Italy**
Year: **2001**

Prior to the 2001 G8
Summit in which the
leaders of Canada, France,
Germany, Italy, Japan,
Russia, the United
Kingdom, and the United
States met in Genova, Italy,
Silvio Berlusconi govern-
ment claimed it would
guarantee the right to
peaceful protest.
However, this claim was
swept aside during the
resulting, widespread
demonstrations. Clashes
between the police and
protestors resulted in 482
injuries and 280 arrests.
Perhaps the most dramatic
moment occurred when
Italian police shot dead
activist Carlo Giuliani. The
caption of this poster reads,
"We have seen Genova."
The counter spaces of the
"8" have been replaced by
stylized illustrations of
police with clubs raised.

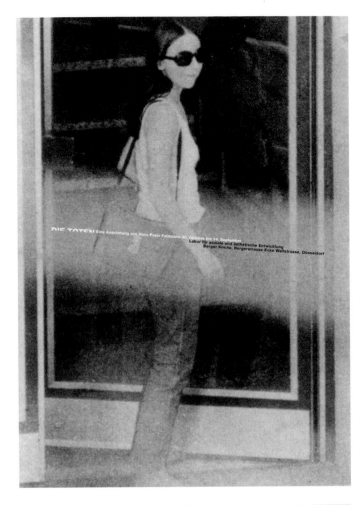

Title: **Die Toten**
Format: **Poster series**
Art Director/Designer:
Fons Hickmann
Client: **No client**
Country: **Germany**
Year: **Unknown**

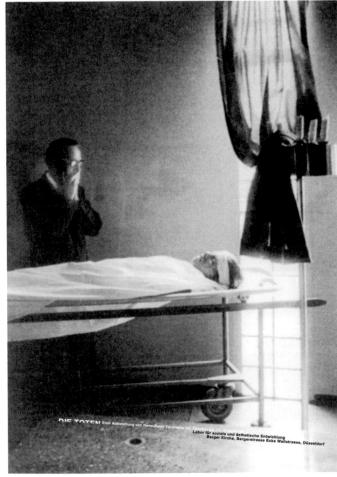

These posters announce
an exhibit by Hans-Peter
Feldman based on a period
of RAF (Red Army Faction)
left-wing terrorism in
West Germany from 1968
to 1985. One poster uses
a photograph of RAF
member Elisabeth von
Dyck moments before the
German Secret Service
killed her in their attempt
to arrest her. The other is
a photograph of RAF
member Petra Schelm's
dead body attended by
his father. Each poster
announces the times and
dates of the exhibit, along
with the exhibit title "Die
Toten," which means
"The Dead."

Title: **links/rechts**
Format: **Poster**
Art Director/Designers:
**Lars Harmsen,
Ulrich Weiß, Lutz Wahler,
Michael Lutz**
Client: **Gruppe 10**
Country: **Germany**
Year: **1994**

Wer nicht wählt, wählt rechtsextrem,
wer rechtsextrem wählt, wählt besser nicht.

Every other month Gruppe
10 sends a magazine, a
poster collection, a slide-
show etc. to its subscribers.
This image is part of a
collection of posters that was
sent out a few weeks before
the chancellor election in
Germany. The title plays on
the words "left" and "right,"
to illustrate that people
don't know what they are
voting for.

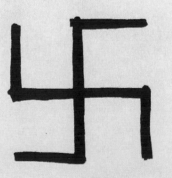

THE SILENT MAJORITY

Title: **The Silent Majority**
Format: **Poster**
Art Director/Designer:
Primo Angeli
Photographer: **Lars Speyer**
Client: **No client**
Country: **Italy**
Year: **1969**

The headline of this poster refers to comments made by President Nixon in which he demeaned protesters by deeming those who supported the war as "the silent majority." This designer proposes that the true silent majority is composed of soldiers buried in the Colma military cemetery in California under tombstones bearing numbers rather than names.

Title: **Resist Empire**
Format: **Buttons**
Art Director/Designer:
Kyle Goen
Client: **No client**
Country: **USA**
Year: **2004**

This series of buttons is intended to encourage people to read the works by the authors featured. Unfortunately, identifying stickers are placed inside the buttons, which only helps the owner of the button. It's the long running Blackgama mink ad problem—it only works if the photograph is of someone instantly recognizable, a real legend.

(top left to right) Amy Goodman, Arundhati Roy, Tariq Ali *(bottom left to right)* Angela Y. Davis, Noam Chomsky, Edward Said

Title: **React Manual**
Format: **Booklet**
Art Director/Designers:
Tom Sieu, John Givens
Client: **Amnesty International**
Country: **USA**
Year: **2003**

The React Manual for Amnesty was an activism tool kit designed to urge sixteen- to twenty-five-year-olds to stand up against oppression and repressive government. The kit included information on how individuals could get involved, as well as a CD containing messaging templates, such as letters to congressmen and women, and banners that people could customize and use.

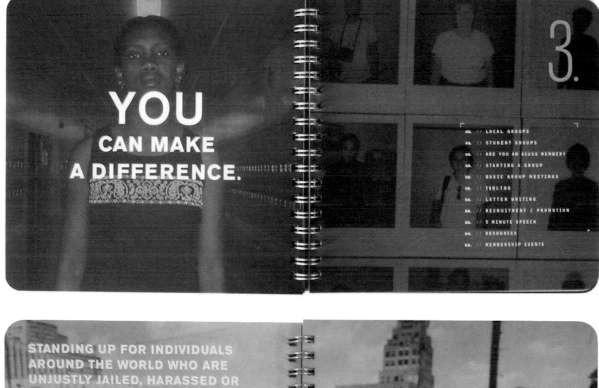

Title: **Rage Against the Machine**
Format: **CD cover**
Illustrator: **Eric Drooker**
Client: **Epic Records/Sony**
Country: **USA**
Year: **1997**

This illustration, titled "Police Riot," was originally created in 1988 as a reaction to an attempt by the New York City Police to impose a curfew on Thompkins Square Park (in Manhattan), an action that caused a large riot. Rage Against the Machine, one of the most radical and successful left-wing rock groups of the '90s reused the art on their CD and VHS.

Title: *Bully*
Format: **Book**
Designer/Illustrator:
Sue Coe
Client: **Four Walls
Eight Windows**
Country: **USA**
Year: **2004**

Like Hieronymus Bosch,
the gothic painter known
as "The master of the
monstrous, the discoverer
of the unconscious," this
artist depicts hell and
oppression around a world
created by a superpower.
Despite working in the
"dark ages," Bosch also
saw a vision of a beautiful
paradise. Sue Coe is much
more realistic.

Title: *Arkzin*
Format: **Magazine**
Art Director/Designers:
**Dejan Krsić, Dejan
Dragosavac Rutta**
Client: *Arkzin*
Country: **Croatia**
Year: **1997**

Arkzin started as an
antiwar campaign
newsletter when the wars
broke out in the former
Yugoslavia. It has since
developed into a
mainstream magazine
devoted to the civil,
cultural, and alternative
political scene.

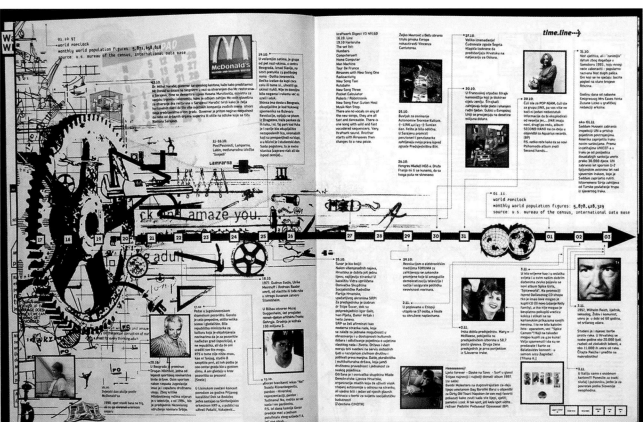

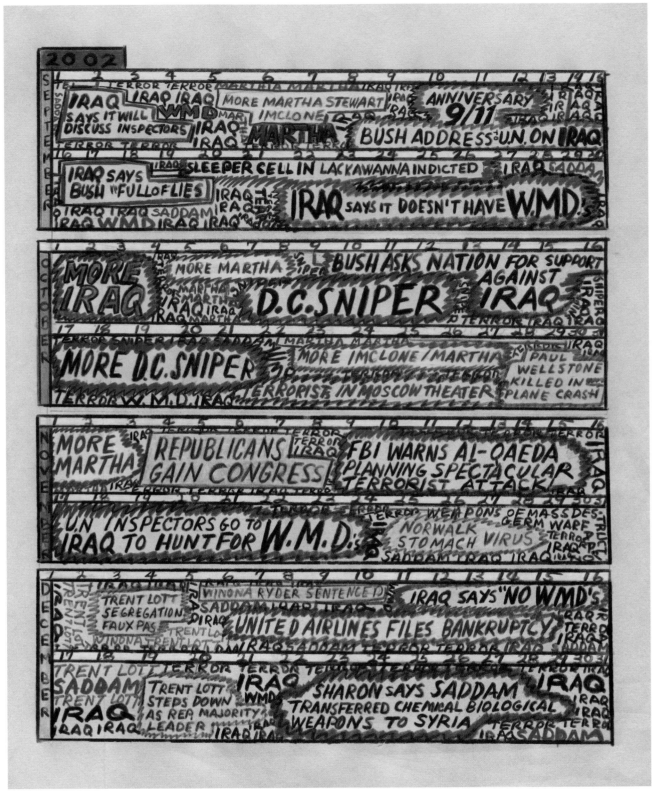

Title: **All the News That Fits**
Format: **Visual essay**
Art Director/Designer:
Paula Scher
Client: *Print* magazine
Country: **USA**
Year: **2001–2003**

This visual essay, which
appeared in *Print*
magazine, records in a
personal and powerful way,
the texture of the news
before and after 9/11. The
author, Paula Scher,
observes "The news
abruptly switched from a
background of sex to a
background of terror,
without missing a beat."
The image shown is only a
small portion of the work.

Title: Illustrated Letters
Format: Electronic images
Art Director/Designer:
Nikola Djurek
Client: Rick Valicenti/Thirst
Country: Croatia
Year: 2003–2004

The artist used photographs that he took of the television news over a two year time period to create an interpretative alphabet that shows the current world we live in from his perspective. The images are posted and sold through the website: play-rickvalicenti.com.

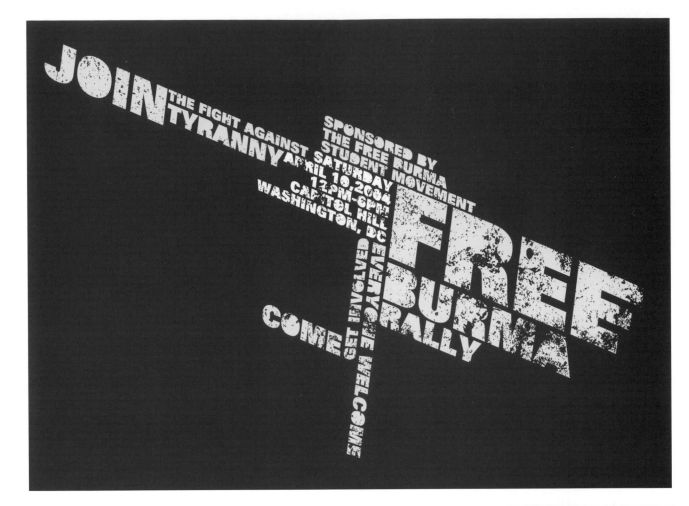

Title: **Free Burma**
Format: **Poster/Flyer**
Art Director/Designer:
James Song
Client: **No client**
Country: **USA**
Year: **2004**

The image of a machine gun is suggestively created by the typography in this poster for a rally sponsored by the Free Burma Student Movement in Washington, D.C. The current leader of Burma came into power through a military coup that provoked student opposition.

Title: **Left Right Boom**
Format: **Poster**
Art Director/Designer:
Yarom Vardimon
Client: **Museum of the Seam, Jerusalem**
Country: **Israel**
Year: **2002**

The typographic rhythms of this poster call for tolerance and reflect the militaristic state of affairs in Israel. This piece was displayed outside the German Reichstag as part of the Coexistence Internal traveling exhibition in 2003.

Hijoputa!

Arial Symbol www.lsdspace.com

Arial Symbol www.lsdspace.com Robin Nicholas and Patricia Saunders

Title: Postcards:
Political Types
Format: Postcards
Art Director/Designers:
Sonia Freeman,
Gabriel Freeman
Client: LSDspace
Country: Spain
Year: Unknown

This variation of Arial appropriates a loaded symbol to evoke power and fear. Along with an expletive, these cards read, "No one must be authorized in spoiling what nature has created for the sake of racial evolution. Your highest purpose in life should be to better maintain this evolution toward a better, stronger, and beautiful humanity."

Nadie debe ser autorizado en malograr lo que la naturaleza creó en aras de la evolución racial. Tu más elevado propósito en la vida ha de ser el de mantener dicha evolución hacia una humanidad mejor, más fuerte y bella. La pureza de la más elevada de las razas es el requisito esencial para cualquier evolución superior. (III. TEN FE EN TU RAZA)

Raza

Arial Symbol www.lsdspace.com

xix futuro

xo ex xólo pobrexx ecoxómicx (mexox de ux dólxr xl díx). "xer pobre ex texer hxmbre, cxrecer de cobijo y ropx, extxr exfermo y xo xer xtexdido, xer iletrxdo y xo recibir formxcióx; xupoxe vulxerxbilidxd xxte xxx xdverxidxdex y x mexudo pxdecer mxl trxto y exclusóx de lxx ixxtitucioxex".

xxox futurx (dexpuéx de pxul rexxer)   www.bxbxpxce.com

Title: Postcards:
Political Types
Format: Postcards
Art Director/Designers:
Sonia Freeman,
Gabriel Freeman
Client: LSDspace
Country: Spain
Year: Unknown

Futura suggests concepts of legibility and coherence, concepts associated with order and rationality. This font becomes illegible and therefore irrational when the letters "s," "a," and "n" are crossed out. These read, "Fraternity, liberty, equality, humanity" and "Without future...to be poor is to be hungry, to lack shelter and clothing is to be illiterate and not receive information."

XBCDEFGHIJKLM
MÑOPQRXTUVW
XYZ. XXXX FUTURX

fraterxidxd
libertxd
iguxldxd
ixhumxxidxd

derechox humxxox = xxxx futurx   www.bxbxpxce.com

POP QUIZ

BY OPEN, N.Y. FOR MOVEON.ORG

Q: WHO SAID "I WILL LEAVE NO CHILD BEHIND" AND THEN CUT $6 BILLION OF EDUCATION FUNDING?

SOURCE: The New York Times

A: GEORGE W. BUSH.

Q: WHO PROMISED $400 BILLION FOR MEDICARE AND THEN BUDGETED ONLY $40 BILLION?

SOURCES: speech 1/29/03 vs. Federal Budget 2004

A: GEORGE W. BUSH.

Q: WHO SUPPORTED A PAY CUT FOR U.S. TROOPS IN THE MIDDLE EAST?

SOURCE: San Francisco Chronicle

A: GEORGE W. BUSH.

Q: WHO WAS THE FIRST U.S. PRESIDENT TO ABANDON AN INTERNATIONAL NUCLEAR ARMS TREATY?

SOURCE: CNN

A: GEORGE W. BUSH.

Q: WHAT'S WRONG WITH THIS PICTURE?

A:

Title: Pop Quiz
Format: Television ad
Art Director/Designers:
Scott Stowell,
Cara Brower,
Susan Barber,
Kate Kittredge
Client: MoveOn.org
Country: USA
Year: 2003

This television spot was created for a contest called "Bush in 30 Seconds" run by the activist organization MoveOn.org. The main goal of the piece was to reach out to Bush supporters with hard facts about the Bush Administration in the hopes of prompting some of them to think twice about who they would vote for in the next election.

Title: Nobody
Format: Yard sign
Art Director/Designer:
Tyler Galloway
Client: No client
Country: USA
Year: 2000

This yard sign proposes that every person contributes in some way to the enrichment of the community. The designer muses, "Imagine participating in free, networked associations of neighbors, neighborhoods, and cities. No hierarchy. No politicians. No hidden agendas. Just direct input. Direct decisions. Direct democracy."

NO MORE BU--SH--!

FERMEZ LA BUSH!

Title: No More Bu__Sh__!
Fermez La Bush!
Format: Bumper sticker
Art Director/Designer:
Erena Rae
Client: No client
Country: USA
Year: 1991/2003

These bumper stickers use two variations on presidents' names: one, in reference to George H. Bush, is scatological; the other is a response to the boycotting of French wine during George W. Bush's administration. In this instance, "Fermez la Bush" ("Close your "mouth") can be read as a message to the French or the American public.

Title: Bush
Format: **Poster**
Art Director/Designer:
Andrew Lewis
Client: **No client**
Country: **USA**
Year: **2002**

The United States sinks
into darkness as a result of
the Bush Presidency.

LIGHT UP THE SKY

The Republicans have every right to meet and choose their candidate in our city without abuse. At the same time, their convention creates an opportunity for all of us to express our disagreement with the culture of militarization and violence that our current leaders represent. It is time to change the meanspirited and abrasive tone of our civic discourse. We need an alternative to the harsh and degrading words and images that have filled our consciousness since the war began.

AN ALTERNATIVE RESPONSE THAT REQUIRES NO PERMIT

On August 30, from dusk to dawn, all citizens who wish to end the Bush presidency can use light as our metaphor. We can gather informally all over the city with candles, flashlights and plastic wands to silently express our sorrow over all the innocent deaths the war has caused. We can gather in groups or march in peaceful confrontation without violence. Violence will only convince the undecided electorate to vote for Bush. Not a word needs to be spoken. The entire world will understand our message. Those of us who live here in rooms with windows on the street can keep our lights on through the night. Imagine, it's 2 or 3 in the morning and our city is ablaze with a silent and overwhelming rebuke... *Light transforms darkness.*

FOR UPDATES, LISTEN TO AIR AMERICA WLIB 1190 AM

www.lightupthesky.org

Title: Light Up the Sky
Format: **Poster**
Art Director/Designer:
Milton Glaser
Client: **No client**
Country: **USA**
Year: **2004**

When New York City restricted protesters during the Republican Convention, lighting the city with any means possible became a more viable way of speaking out. "I was thinking about how dreadful the city was going to be during the convention, the rage, the acrimony, the police ... What was needed was a solution that would not create civic disorder." Many protestors participated although media coverage was minimal. It simply didn't have the entertainment value of protestors and police encountering one another.

Title: *The Nation Initiative Buttons*
Format: **Buttons**
Art Director/Designer: **Milton Glaser**
Client: *The Nation*
Country: **USA**
Year: **2003–2004**

The "Dubya" series of buttons was quite popular. John Kerry picked up the theme for a while and used it in his speeches during the campaign.

Title: **Show Your Blue**
Format: **Advertisement**
Art Director/Designer: **Milton Glaser**
Client: *The Nation*
Country: **USA**
Year: **2004**

After the 2004 U.S. presidential election, many hoped that a spirit of cooperation might arise. However, the "red" and "blue" states became more polarized than ever. These buttons are a call to action for all those opposed to the spirit and stance of the Bush Administration.

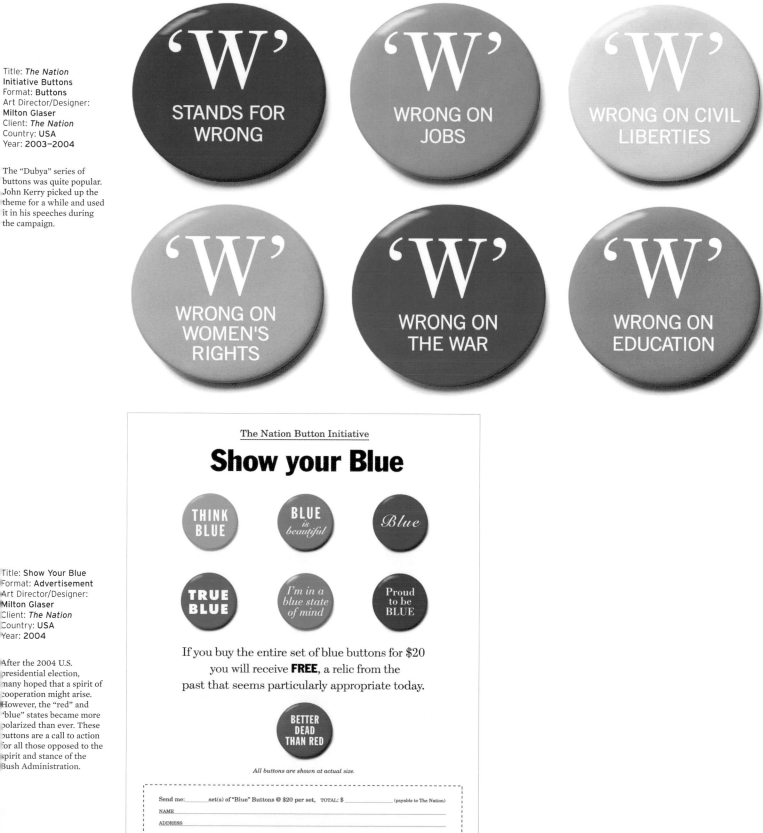

'W' STANDS FOR WRONG

'W' WRONG ON JOBS

'W' WRONG ON CIVIL LIBERTIES

'W' WRONG ON WOMEN'S RIGHTS

'W' WRONG ON THE WAR

'W' WRONG ON EDUCATION

The Nation Button Initiative

Show your Blue

THINK BLUE

BLUE *is beautiful*

Blue

TRUE BLUE

I'm in a blue state of mind

Proud to be BLUE

If you buy the entire set of blue buttons for $20 you will receive **FREE**, a relic from the past that seems particularly appropriate today.

BETTER DEAD THAN RED

All buttons are shown at actual size.

Send me:_____ set(s) of "Blue" Buttons @ $20 per set, TOTAL: $ _____ (payable to The Nation)
NAME
ADDRESS

CITY   STATE   ZIP
Please send check or cash to : The Nation, Nation Building, 33 Irving Place, 8th Floor, New York, NY 10003

VOTE against bush in november

how do you sleep at night? knowing you are responsible for the death of over **8,800** Iraqi civilians and the death of over **680** American soldiers; knowing you turned the US budget surplus into a deficit of over **$520** billion; knowing 2.4 million Americans have lost their jobs during your administration; knowing your efforts have weakened **200** public health and environmental laws;

Title: **How Do You Sleep at Night?**
Format: **Poster**
Art Director/Designer:
Ginny Warren
Client: **Invent**
Country: **USA**
Year: **2004**

In raising the question, "How do you sleep at night?" this designer hopes to evoke images of war and death in relationship to President Bush, suggesting that if he had a conscience, he would not be able to sleep at night.

Ceci n'est pas un terroriste.

Title: **Ceci n'est pas un terroriste.**
Format: **Magazine ad**
Art Director/Designers:
**Mateja D. Zavrl,
Robert Kržmančič**
Client: *Mladina* magazine
Country: **Slovenia**
Year: **2002**

This ad, created for the Slovenian political weekly *Mladina* magazine, presumes that the magazine's readership is familiar with Magritte's painting, *Ceci n'est pas une pipe*, in which the artist asks his audience to question what we accept as reality by presenting a painting of a pipe and titling it "This is not a pipe." In this case, the title reads "This is not a terrorist."

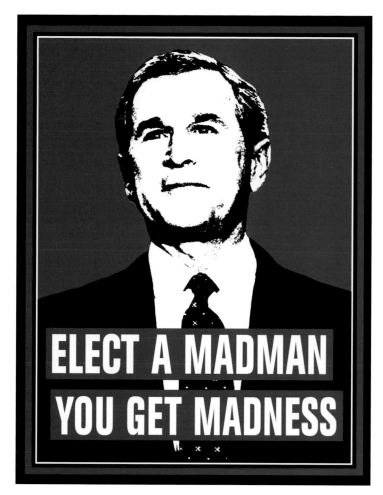

Title: **Elect a Madman**
–You Get Madness
Format: **Poster**
Art Director/Designer:
Kyle Goen
Client: **No client**
Country: **USA**
Year: **2004**

The style of this poster (shown below at the Stay Gold Gallery/Art Space in Brooklyn, New York) was created in response to the U.S. presidential election derives in part from Barbara Kruger's signature red and black works, while the text is a borrowed phrase from Alice Walker's 1989 novel, *The Temple of my Familiar*. "President nuts. Can't they see anything? Elect a madman. What do you get? Madness."

Title: **The Moron Terror**
Format: **Poster**
Art Director/Designer:
Adrienne Burk
Client: **No client**
Country: **USA**
Year: **2004**

In this poster, "The War on Terror," a phrase used incessantly by the Bush Administration, is transformed and coupled with the infamous image of President Bush in his flight suit announcing that the war in Iraq was over. The poster was used at anti-Iraq War protests.

Title: **Richie Bush**
Format: **Comic book**
Art Director/Designer:
Peter Kuper
Client: **No client**
Country: **USA**
Year: **2003**

This comic book, based on an earlier comic character Richie Rich, was used at 2004 presidential election events. The author notes, "The surreal level of lies, hubris, and verbal pretzels we've been asked to swallow by the Bush Administration made the comic book an appropriate vehicle for characterizing them." Inside is a comic homage to Snoopy, Charlie Brown, and Woodstock. Because of this, the issue was seized in 2004 by U.S. Customs because it constituted "clearly piratical copies". After complains and discussions about the First Amendment of free speech, the US Customs changed their decision. *(top left and right)*

Title: **Bushit**
Format: **Die-cut cardboard**
Art Director/Designer:
Mirko Ilić
Copywriter: **Daniel Young**
Client: **Daniel Young**
Country: **USA**
Year: **2004**

Created for shock value, die-cut cardboard was used to create a disconcerting 3-D effect. The pieces were distributed widely on the streets and sidewalks of New York City by the designer and creative director, their collegues, and friends before the 2004 Republican National Convention. *(bottom left)*

Title: **Dum Gum**
Format: **Chewing gum packaging**
Art Director/Designer:
Haley Johnson
Client: **Blue Q**
Country: **USA**
Year: **2004**

The artist speculates who is really dumb: President Bush or the gullible public who buy his lies? *(bottom right)*

Title: **Republican Rage**
Format: **Poster**
Art Director/Designer:
Ward Sutton
Client: **No client**
Country: **USA**
Year: **2001**

Elephants never forget and neither do Republicans, according to the results of the 2000 election. The artist believes right-wing anger and a mob-rules mentality forced Democratic presidential candidate, Al Gore, into the position of loser. *(top)*

Title: **The Worst Political Ads in America Event**
Format: **Logo**
Art Director/Designers:
**Bill Thorburn,
Travis Olson**
Client: **Growth & Justice**
Country: **USA**
Year: **2004**

Growth & Justice, a nonpartisan public policy institute, stands for civil dialogue. This logo designed for their "The Worst Political Ads in America" fund-raiser plays off the egocentric showoff as well as political parties and their advertising agencies. *(bottom left)*

Title: **Ceci n'est pas une comic**
Format: **Magazine comic**
Art Director/Designer:
Nicholas Blechman
Illustration: **Peter Kuper**
Client: *NOZONE*
Country: **USA**
Year: **2003**

The comic created for the Empire issue of *NOZONE* magazine plays with the notion of reality compared to what the Bush Administration espouses. The comic borrows images from Magritte's *Ceci n'est pas une pipe* painting, a surreal icon. *(bottom right)*

Title: **We Need
More Party Animals**
Format: **Poster**
Art Director/Designer:
Thomas Porostocky
Client: *Repeat/Defeat*
Newspaper
Country: **USA**
Year: **2004**

This poster was designed as
a playful protest against the
limited choices imposed by
the two-party political
system in America.

© tomi porostocky 2004

THE D
OF DIS

BY TONY KUSHNER

At the beginning of Stendhal's *The Charterhouse of Parma*, the French army arrives in Milan, whose citizens, under the despotic rule of the Holy Roman Empire, "were still subject to certain minor monarchical restrictions that continued to vex them. For instance," Stendhal writes:

> "the Archduke, who resided in Milan and governed in the name of his cousin the [Holy Roman] Emperor, had conceived the lucrative notion of speculating in wheat.

Consequently, no peasant could sell his crop until His Highness's granaries were full.

In May 1796, three days after the entry of the French, a young miniaturist named Gros, slightly mad and subsequently famous, arrived with the army and overheard talk in the great Caffè dei Servi (fashionable at the time) of the exploits of the Archduke, who happened to be extremely fat. Snatching up the list of ices stamped on a sheet of coarse yellow paper, he drew on the back a French

ESIGN SENT

soldier thrusting his bayonet into the obese Archduke's belly: instead of blood out poured an incredible quantity of grain. The idea of caricature or cartoon was unknown in this nation of wary despotism. The sketch Gros had left on the table of the Caffè dei Servi seemed a miracle from Heaven; it was printed overnight, and twenty thousand copies were sold the next day.

This image shares with other successful instances of graphic dissent at least three characteristics: It is shocking, it is clever—even funny in a grim sort of way—and its meaning is instantly intelligible. And perhaps it shares one other character-

istic: It is, or at least it seems to be, samizsdat, dangerous, forbidden. Resistance is sending up a signal flare in the darkness. A scrap of torn menu has been left on a café table, left behind for others to find, others who know what the artist knows—that a violent, unjust, criminal order is overdue for abolishment. Some galling truth that has yet to be organized, formulated, that can't yet be spoken out loud, that can be only grumbled and whispered, some truth that lies imprisoned beneath the surface of public discourse is suddenly, finally liberated, shouted at great volume, a cry of rebellion carrying everywhere at once, a cry all the more powerful for being entirely silent, expressed by a cartoon, entirely visual, needing no words, as if to say, by

saying nothing at all: "We all know this truth, all of us have always known what's represented here, that's why it's so recognizable. And it's time to declare the secret openly in public places; it's time to act." As Freud warns us, when the repressed returns, it does so with immense force.

Stendhal chooses Antoine-Jean Gros's little act of graphic design/terrorism to emblematize a turning point of political consciousness, the awakening of an oppressed people to an awareness that "whatever it had hitherto respected was sovereignly absurd and on occasion odious." It had waited in everyone's mind, this public execution of the tyrant, this goring of a greedy aristocrat; it needed only Gros's impulsive, casual, almost-accidental gesture of public articulation, and the collective mind and spirit of the people leapt forward in a lightning rush to greet it, to embrace it, and to act on the Promethean freedom fire it delivered to them. Stendhal is describing one of those images everyone has encountered at least once in his or her life—an image on a poster, brand-new yet long-expected, possessing the power of the Uncanny, as if a complete stranger on the street had stepped up to you and spoken clearly something deeply familiar but also deeply private, something you believed only you or very few others like you believed. Miraculous indeed. The political is the arena of the miraculous, where the collective and the communal, so routinely repressed, so viciously suppressed, stages its returns, where eternal truths and immortal edifices can dissolve in an eye blink, in historical time, where change rather than stasis is the only constant. Marianne Moore describes the miracle of the political perfectly: "That which it is impossible to force, it is impossible to hinder."

It is even more of a miracle that the act of forcing the impossible is, in the history of political revolution, often catalyzed by something as flimsy as a poster plastered on a wall—the perfect poster on the perfect wall at the perfect moment. What's miraculous is not that great graphic design, employing shock, wit, and clarity borne of urgency, can move people to action, to acts of courage and sacrifice, overcoming habit and fear. Art can do that; art is always having those sorts of effects. Art can't change anything except people—but art changes people, and people can make everything change.

What's truly miraculous is that, as hard as it is to make the perfect poster—and it must be immensely hard—someone nearly always seems to be on hand to do the job when the time demands it. Consider the miracle of John Heartfield, Käthe Kollwitz, Aleksander Rodchenko, Casimir Malevich, Vladimir Tatlin, the designers of ACT UP's SILENCE=DEATH, and the artists who edited and are represented in this volume. The time arrives for a silent truth to become a public truth, a collective truth; the pressure of great human need bids the time arrive. Human need conjures up the messianic moment—at least some of the time it does.

"No More War" (Poster)
Käthe Kollwitz, 1924

Is there a dismal history to be written of embryonic political movements aborted for want of a great graphic designer? One ought to be careful about claiming too much for art, but fires die for lack of kindling. So I suspect that there may be such a history, though I'm not sure I want anyone to bother unearthing it.

Returning to the passage from *Charterhouse*, it should be pointed out that Gros sketches his caricature three days after the French have taken Milan, and the Archduke's reign is already over; rather than simply helping overturn a greedy tyrant, Gros is also doing his part in cementing French domination of the Milanese, replacing Austro-Hungarian/Spanish domination. Stendhal's infallible irony drew him to this, a fat pig of an archduke being skewered graphically by a caricaturist whose name means "big"—and who did, in fact, become "famous" as an anti-Romanticist conservative painter whose epic canvasses flattered newly minted emperors and kings (and who finally committed suicide).

It's hardly news: Politics is impure, political actors human and fallible, and the battles of opposites are never sharp edged. Twenty-first-century admirers of great political graphic design can't banish an uneasiness in appreciating design's power to catalyze change. We've seen too often how great design successfully sells monstrous lies, and we know how closely related to the whole process of selling and branding, of merchandising and commodifying, how intimately related to business, to commerce, all graphic art is. The marketplace created graphic design, its vocabulary, its ether. This is to say nothing more than that an appreciation of the progressive power of great political graphic design leads us to an appreciation of how inescapable the language of oppression and exploitation is, even in the struggle against oppres-

The Bug As Vermin
Exterminator (Magazine)
John Heartfield, 1933

sion—an appreciation shaped more elegantly by the French than by any other culture, from Stendhal through Proust through Althusser. This awareness can lead to despair, if one concludes that change is impossible, or to hope, if one concludes that every phenomenon, including language, including the language of oppression, carries within itself the seeds of its own unraveling.

So great is our knowledge, in the early years of the twenty-first century, of all that has come before us, so vast is our experience of both human success and also staggering, holocaustic failure, and so sophisticated is our understanding of how little we understand, how vaguely we understand, that a toxic cynicism pervades our spirit, shutting down our capacity for faith, for hope, for imagining change—and consequently shutting down our passion, our imagination. These posters, these works of art, have a restorative power. Each is an argument that stamps itself indelibly in on the soul of the passer-by; accepted or rejected, the argument, the claim, or demand each makes becomes a spark in the dialectical engine of consciousness, of human life. The best of these posters speak with a direct force, past all our qualifying, temporizing, even our scrupling and wisdom, to our passion, our appetite, our starved hunger for communal understanding, for collective agency, for belonging, for justice, and for change.

–Tony Kushner © 2005

Silence=Death (Poster)
Act Up, New York, 1986

Tony Kushner, born in Manhattan in July of 1956, grew up in Lake Charles, Louisiana, where his family moved after inheriting a lumber business. He earned a bachelor's degree from Columbia University and later did postgraduate work at New York University. In the early 1980s, he founded a theater group and began writing and producing plays. In the early 1990s, he scored a monster hit with the epic, seven-hour, two-part, Broadway blockbuster *Angels in America: A Gay Fantasia on National Themes*, which earned a Pulitzer Prize, two Tony Awards, two Drama Desk Awards, the Evening Standard Award, two Olivier Award Nominations, the New York Critics Circle Award, the Los Angeles Drama Critics Circle Award, and the LAMBDA Liberty Award for Drama. This groundbreaking play focuses on three households in turmoil: a gay couple, one of whom has AIDS; a Mormon man coming to terms with his sexuality; and the infamous lawyer Roy Cohn, a historical figure who died of AIDS in 1986, denying his homosexuality all the way to his deathbed. *Newsweek* wrote of *Angels in America:*

"Daring and Dazzling! The most ambitious American play of our time: an epic that ranges from earth to heaven; focuses on politics, sex and religion; transports us to Washington, the Kremlin, the South Bronx, Salt Lake City and Antarctica; deals with Jews, Mormons, WASPs, blacks; switches between realism and fantasy, from the tragedy of AIDS to the camp comedy of drag queens to the death or at least the absconding of God."

DISSE COND

MILTON GLASER INTERVIEWED BY STEVEN HELLER

Heller: In oppressive societies, dissent is alternately called subversion, reaction, blasphemy, and is usually viewed as a criminal act. In the United States, dissent is a positive thing. Would you agree?

Glaser: It depends what the meaning of "positive" is, to paraphrase our former president. Dissent seems to have a liturgical quality, or, at least, a reference to the dogma of the church, and I think the word was used more frequently in that sense than almost any other, where there was a dissent from the agreed-upon conventions of the church by people who wanted to modify or change those conventions.

Heller: You mean the way that Martin Luther launched the Reformation when he nailed his Ninety-Five Theses to the door of the Wittenberg Church?

Glaser: Yes, among others. It seems to me that dissent disagrees with religious dogma as often as it does about political dogma. Although in both cases, they are attempts to deal with existing power.

Heller: Changing an established order is the goal of dissent. But is it done in a constructive or destructive way?

Glaser: It can be either. Dissenters usually have the idea that their dissent is an attempt to improve an existing condition. Although I suppose in the American South, when racist Southerners were demonstrating against the Civil Rights movement, from our point of view, we might say that the reaction was motivated by self-interest rather than a sense of fairness.

Heller: Were they using "dissent" as their operative term, or was it a blatant rejection of the federal government's imposition of equal rights?

Glaser: I'm not sure it's relevant whether people use the word "dissent" or not. They certainly disagreed with the government and an aspect of dissent is disagreement. We like to feel dissent is about a notion of fairness that is being violated by the existing power structure.

Heller: Is fairness the key issue?

Glaser: This notion of fairness may be intrinsic to our species. Adam Cohen in the *New York Times* ["Editorial Observer; What the Monkeys Can Teach Humans About Making America Fairer" – September 21, 2003] wrote about experiments conducted by scientists in Scandinavia with Capuchin monkeys proving that when they were all fed the same kind of food, they were very cooperative and would exchange things for the food that they were given. But as soon as one member of the group was given a delicacy that was considered to be superior to what the rest were

all receiving, the monkeys went crazy. They could not stand the idea that they were not treated equally or fairly. From this, the observation was made, and apparently for the first time, that a sense of fairness is intrinsic to primates, an idea that goes beyond our individual cultures, where it sometimes exists as a precept, but actually is in the racial memory of the species. One can only assume that this structure is a way to promote the survival of the species. So fairness itself may have represented a biological device to protect the species by developing a sense of community.

Heller: But how does this unfold in the face of world behavior where we see various groups subjugate others and, thus, impose unfair conditions on the vanquished? This happens every day. Obviously, unfairness provokes dissent.

Glaser: You wouldn't need a sense of fairness if the desire for power and the instinct to kill one's enemy were not another very fundamental characteristic of primates. Those perceived as not being of the same species, or even the same class, are held in contempt.

Heller: Dissent has long been manifest in a human desire for equality, but it has always been a fight against an overwhelming power that imposes harm on others.

Glaser: Exactly. And of course, when you think of dissenting conditions, there is always a source of power that is instrumental in producing dissent. The reaction of dissent is always in response to a sense of oppression that is experienced by those who dissent.

Heller: Dissent *does* have this positive implication as protest against injustice. But what is good dissent and what is bad dissent?

Glaser: If we characterize dissent as being mere disagreement we easily lapse into the eye-of-the-beholder argument: Is my view equal to your view? What is a good act as opposed to an evil act? You can get very Talmudic and convoluted in this ancient philosophical argument.

But I think that there is some sense of righteousness in dissenting opinion, and that is generally the reason that it comes into being. We do know that, inevitably, powerful institutions begin to oppress those who have less power. This seems to be as fundamental a characteristic of the species as fairness. So in response to the whole notion of unassailable power, dissent is a positive response and, as the button I designed says, "dissent protects democracy."

Heller: But as you have noted, dissent also protects undemocratic ideas. We are in political milieu today where fundamentalists have transformed their dissent into power to overturn laws and social contracts that we've accepted as part of a liberal agenda for much of the mid- to late twentieth century.

Glaser: Again, it all comes down to the difficulty of deciding what is true, what is false, what is right, what is wrong, which is never an easy question. But we do know that there is, at least, an ethical core to the idea of dissent, and that dissent is very necessary because of the institutional instinct to move toward a totalitarian position—that authority, whatever its source, religious, political or academic, always attempts to marginalize people and movements considered to be deviant or not congruent with their objectives.

Heller: Isn't it interesting that the word "propaganda," which is a tool of both power and dissent, also stems from a religious root—the propagation of the faith, the Jesuits whose mission it was to make sure that people who questioned the faith were brought back into line?

Glaser: Well, it continues to be one of the problems of power. Because even though religion is theoretically an attempt to improve the condition of mankind, to make things better—to diminish unfairness—what we discover that, like politics, religion is susceptible to the same manifestations. Because of that, the history of religion is frequently bloody, unfair, and conspiratorial. So, at a certain point in your life you just begin to question this idea of absolute belief when it stems from any single source, and you become, inevitably, more skeptical and perhaps more open-minded about the characteristics of belief, and you recognize that all belief finally represents a limitation in thinking. Because when you believe something, your mind is no longer open to alternatives, and once that happens, the mind stops operating and goes on autopilot.

Heller: So does this mean that dissent should be a perpetual condition whereby you're always questioning authority or dogma?

Glaser: If you're in a constant state of dissent, you're in trouble because you believe that dissent is the only position to take. In that belief, you have become encapsulated in your own convictions. So the dissenting personality, which we may be critical of to some degree, is one that always, in a kind of knee-jerk way, says "no" to any expression of belief that is alternative to their own. That's not, to me, the great expression of dissent. I think dissent has a more positive side.

Heller: Is dissent sometimes a lofty word for complaint?

Glaser: In part, and of course we all know people who believe nothing is ever right; it doesn't matter what the subject matter is. The meal they had, the movie they saw, the political system they're living in—nothing is acceptable. The sadness about that, of course, is that these people are not choosing their responses. These people are not choosing their response (although I don't know to what degree any of us choose anything freely), but are victims of a personality that simply says no to everything.

Heller: Dissent can be curtailed by official decrees and regulations. If dissent offers positive alternatives, why is it so terrifying?

Glaser: The loss of power is terrifying to all of us. If you're the king, and you have a life for yourself and your cronies that is very happy and satisfying, and all of a sudden people are turning out by thousands in the street and you realize you could lose everything, well, you're not going to leave quietly. So, in the case of institutions like the church or political systems, those in power spend their life holding on to it, and those who threaten that power are in for a very hard time, depend-

Early Christian Symbol from Roman Catacombs, at the time Christians were persecuted.

"Unite or Die!"
Benjamin Fraklin, 1776

Citizens of Boston, disguised as Native Americans, boarding ships in Boston Harbor and throwing chests of tea overboard.
Engraver Daniel Berger, 1784

From *Los Desastres De La Guerra*
Goya, 1810

ing on just how much pressure the power can wield.

Heller: Under the umbrella of dissent, there is peaceful and violent dissent. Which is the most effective?

"King Louis Phillipe" (Caricature)
Honore Daumier, 1832

Glaser: These choices are essentially situational. Sometimes quiet dissent, or non-violence, is very powerful and works very well. One of the reasons it works is because the dissenters cannot be stigmatized so easily by the official power. When the dissent is peaceful, it is more difficult to call demonstrators hoodlums, or communists, or even left-wingers. Of course, Gandhi and Martin Luther King recognized that fact. Power stigmatizes those who dissent by calling them irresponsible and dangerous. Expressions of violence justify violent responses by the established power. It's one of the reasons why people who dissent have to be thoughtful about the mode of dissent in order to accomplish their goals.

Heller: Dissent tends to start small and build, whether it's at a grass-roots level or in an urban context. As you're describing it, peaceful dissent begets more peaceful dissent. But how does one induce others, through communications and design, to become part of a particular groundswell of dissent?

"You've been mumbling 1812 under your breath long enough..." (from *The History of Holy Russia*)
Gustave Dore, 1854

Glaser: Generally, people respond to powerful imagery and words that contain an appeal to justice.

Heller: Is dissent, however, sometimes about fashion?

Glaser: As you recall, we had an evening where we discussed dissent [AIGA/New York's "Hell No" – Spring 2003, and "Hell Yes" – Spring 2004], and one of the things I observed was how ineffective so much dissent is. It can be a way of positioning the self in some situations. Coolness is attached to being a dissenter; the idea of opposing the existing culture is attractive to a lot of young people who want to overthrow their parents or their history, or identify themselves as being autonomous, whatever. In those cases dissent can be both personally satisfying and fashionable. Sneaker manufacturers, among others, have taken great advantage of appearing to represent a counterculture. Can you imagine a sneaker being counterculture?

The busts of policemen are shown as part of an image of the Haymarket Massacre (May 4, 1886 in Chicago) in which police charged labor movement rioters who were demanding eight-hour work days. The event was memorialized by May Day; the government then enacted Labor Day, which could only be interpreted as an effort to obscure the history of what management did to laborers.
Illustrator unknown, 1886

Heller: Ever since the 1950s when teenagers were targeted as a viable market, there have been attempts to persuade them through advertising (propaganda) to buy into and from the respective manufacturers who want their dollars, which includes giving the consumer distinguishing characteristics, like the illusion that they are rebels. But isn't it a fact that dissent usually emerges from the youthful generation?

Glaser: Of course, and certain products now use the idea of the revolution symbolically in urging kids to define their character by buying a product. And that's one of the saddest expressions of dissent that one could imagine.

Heller: Throughout the twentieth century and into the twenty-first, there have been corporations, and the individuals who run them, who have exhibited lofty social and political consciousnesses, and have contributed to various causes, and even supported dissent toward government policies. How do you feel about advertising that's created for a particular product, such as Benetton, Kenneth Cole, or Ben & Jerry's, that use their products as kind of soapboxes for dissent (and advocacy)? Do the waters get muddied there?

Glaser: I think they do get muddied. In a democracy, there must be options within the culture for this kind of expression. But the truth of the matter is that it is the system itself that establishes the values of any culture. Our system believes in materialism and affluence as the fundamental aspirations of society. It is also possible for a democracy to become totalitarian. Witness what's going on right now, where the American people have been victimized into thinking that the ruling class represents their interests. Both education and journalism have failed us in this regard. Belief systems are self-generating. In a democracy, the mythology of democracy must be maintained. We cannot afford to feel that we are warlike, unfair, racist, or so on. But whenever those manifestations occur we deflect them because we must believe our own historical mythology. When we see industrialists giving money to good causes, it confirms our sense of democracy.

Heller: But does it represent dissent, or does it represent something else?

Glaser: Very often, it represents an attempt to demonstrate a concern for "higher values." The oil and tobacco companies are constantly supporting artistic events. The Metropolitan Opera, the Whitney, the Metropolitan Museum of Art are supported by the most pernicious corporations. Do these powerful corporations really care about art?

Heller: I think they come to care deeply about it because of the investment potential. They also care about it because it gives them a pedigree and throws them into a cultural surround that is not simply dollars-and-cents and an exploitation of the working class. It gives them cultural credibility and cultural profit.

Glaser: Perhaps it's like those patrons during the Renaissance who appear at the bottom right and left of many religious paintings. Of course, the love of Jesus was, in fact, the defining characteristic of social life in that society. The defining characteristic today is how much money you have. Instead of buying another Rolls Royce, you can buy a Matisse, and that immediately gives you some kind of status.

Heller: But in terms of dissent, have you ever been involved with individuals who seem kind of like they're going against their own self-interest by supporting the interest of righteous or controversial causes?

Glaser: Oh, I don't know. I've met a lot of nuts in dissenting conditions. I've met a lot of marvelous people. The mix is not necessarily uniform. There's a difference between righteousness and self-righteousness, but it's very difficult sometimes to see where one lapses into the other. I think fundamentally, the people whom I know who are dissenters have a sense of justice; they care about the nature of society. Part of the characteristic of dissent when it's at its best is fueled by empathy, and it's fueled by the idea that other people matter, and that if somebody is hurt or victimized, we are all hurt or victimized.

Heller: Since the '60s when the Situationalists in France began to critique commercial culture through art and design, dissenting groups have co-opted mainstream culture's commercial icons. *Adbusters* magazine is a good example of "culture jamming," or obstructing the free flow of commercial advertising by intercepting and altering their messages on billboards and other media. These are guerilla tactics designed to overtly and subliminally interfere with business as usual. But in recent years the advertising industry has adopted very similar guerilla methods (as though they stole a page from the *Adbusters* manual). How does this now fit into the strategy of dissent? Does it neutralize one of the tools in such a way as to make it more difficult to create effective propaganda for dissent?

Glaser: There are many brilliant people in the world of advertising who understand the power of co-option. They have no sense of shame about these things. So any idea that succeeds will be promptly stolen and used against you.

Heller: Let's discuss the art of dissent—which is, of course, the topic of this book—and the role of the designer as a propagator of dissent. True dissenters are activists. Is creating a poster, button, or ad campaign real activism?

Glaser: It's certainly a form of activism. Should designers be more involved in this activism than others? For years, my response was that a designer's role is not any different from that of any good citizen. From my point of view, good citizens are those who participate in democracy and who express their point of view, and who realize they have a role to play in the life of their time. Being a designer doesn't suggest that you have any *more* responsibility. We all have the responsibility to be good citizens. We can either embrace that responsibility or withdraw from it. The passivity of many Americans has endangered our democracy.

Heller: The role of a designer is clearly to be a good citizen, but how do you feel graphic design as a profession can influence or support dissent?

Glaser: Graphic designers know how to communicate. We've had experience that has trained us for a role in the culture.

One of the things evident in this book is that the work of amateurs very often is as powerful as the work of professionals. Our times are characterized by the erosion, if not the disappearance, of professional practice in certain categories. Almost everyone is obsessed with the idea of design and being a designer.

Heller: So if an amateur can produce a visual message, such as a poster, brochure, or billboard, that will grab us by the lapels and make us think or act, then what does the professional designer bring to the party that the amateur cannot?

Glaser: We are in the midst of this revolutionary change, most profoundly expressed in the Internet, where the blogs now have become an expression of journalism, and where millions of people are now doing reporting, commentary, and editorials, and are beginning to have an effect that official journalism does not have.

In order to become a journalist, for instance, you have to pass a series of tests. After you graduate from journalism school, you become a cub reporter, then you are moved up the scale to reporter, perhaps a columnist or managing editor and, finally, the editor. All of this process imbued you with the history and mythology of journalism as you went along. The same thing happens in design. You go to art school, you learn about form, you study typography, and you learn about color. Then, you learn about the history and continuity of art. After school, you begin by working for somebody, doing low-level tasks, and finally ascending to where you're responsible for communicating something to others.

Heller: There's a man who quietly stands in front of my office one day a week, for the past five years or more holding a poster he's made with a large photograph of a fetus. He wears it as a sandwich board, and it is very hard to ignore that photograph with the headline "Save Life." It's not a particularly clever slogan, but it's a very potent anti-abortion message. He's grabbing some peo-

Simplicissimus
(Magazine)
Thomas Theodore Heine, 1903

Nepszava
(Newspaper Cover)
Biro, 1913

Die Pleite
(Magazine Cover)
George Grosz, 1919

ple by the lapels. What makes him less effective than the graphic designers who are in this book?

Glaser: Who says he is? The real question is: What does it mean when the idea of professional practice is being dramatically eroded by a class of amateurs who want to get into the game, and who, in many cases, are as convincing or as powerful as those who, theoretically, know what they're doing? It's really a question about the nature of professional education. What does it train you for? Of course, among other things, professional practice in the United States also trains you to be a conformist, to listen to the existing rules, to follow orders, and sell products. Education obviously reflects the existing societal values.

Woman suffrage headquarters in Upper Euclid Avenue, Cleveland, Ohio **Photographer unknown,** 1912

Heller: Well, the majority of design professionals do not create art of dissent. But what we're talking about here is a means of combining images and words together, that forces people to move, to act, to respond in some way. Are you saying we don't need all that formal training to successfully make graphic dissent?

Glaser: You have to be smart, and you have to know something about the nature of communication, either by instinct or by training. But of course, what you're suggesting has always been to me the reason for supporting the idea of an ethical practice: If the practice is, in fact, involved in communicating ideas, then you have to be responsible for what you're communicating. I can never separate the consequences of what we do from being in the world of communication. But it seems that, in some areas, people's instincts work without training. Everybody has a screenplay in them, and everybody can do a poster, and everybody can come up with a slogan. Some people are better at it than others. Sometimes, the people who are better at it are professionals. Other times, there are people who are totally untrained who seem to be gifted as observers and commentators.

Civil rights march on Washington, D.C., **Photographer: Warren K. Leffler,** 1963

Heller: Certain posters have iconic resonance that had to do with the context in which they were produced. One such, for example, which was an amateurish-looking piece, is the photographic image of dead women and children murdered by American GIs in the hamlet of My Lai, Vietnam, with the typewritten headline, *Q: And Babies?... A: And Babies!* placed over the image in enlarged typewriter type. You could not wash that poster out of the consciousness. It spoke to a moment. It did so with real pictorial evidence (like Abu Ghraib three decades later), and it became an icon of anti-war resistance. In your experience, what were the one, two, or three most effective graphic campaigns that were either dissent or protest, underscoring a cause or an issue?

Glaser: So much of it is contextual: Where you were, or where the poster was, what was happening, who you were with. All of these experiences about looking at things have so much to do with other things besides the object. I remember on the day before the [Ethel and Julius] Rosenbergs were executed [for espionage in 1953], I was living in Bologna, and all over the town were posters that were put up just with a mug shot of the pair with a protesting phrase: "Don't kill the Rosenbergs." Bologna was always a town with left-wing associations and sympathies. The entire town was plastered (it must have been done by the Communist Party in Bologna) with this picture of two forlorn-looking people who were looking as ordinary and as pathetic as one could imagine. I remember I was overwhelmed. Overwhelmed with the idea that these two inconsequential-looking people, for whatever reason, were being executed in our country. The fact that I was in Bologna, the banality of the picture itself, the fact that it appeared all over the town overnight, made it the single most profoundly dissenting statement I'd ever seen.

Nonetheless, the examples we each cited have very little to do with the design as the graphic object. In fact you could say that a designer could have screwed up those expressions by making them more self-consciously designed. What we were moved by was the poignancy of the event itself.

Heller: What is the purpose of printed dissent? Is the intention to appeal to people who already sympathize with you? Or must it convert those who do not? Whatever the goal, what are the best methods?

Glaser: One has to be very thoughtful about examining the effect of this imagery outside the fact that it's clever, well-done, powerful, and all the rest. Does it work? Is it effective? Are people transformed by it? Does it make them feel different about the subject after they experience it, or does it simply repel them and make them avoid dealing with the subject? Even when I'm moved by some of the most powerful images, I finally have to ask: Can it produce the results it intends?

Heller: I recall another "amateur" anti-Vietnam war poster "War Is Unhealthy for Children and Other Living Things" "designed" by Lorraine Schneider for the Mothers' Mobilization for Peace. It was very effective because the message was not violent and developed an empathetic response. Who couldn't see themselves holding, hanging, or walking with that poster and slogan (if you believed that the Vietnam War was indeed unhealthy)? But can a dissenter change popular opinion through the use of shocking words or images?

Glaser: Well, all of this comes under the general category of consciousness-raising. And sometimes hor-

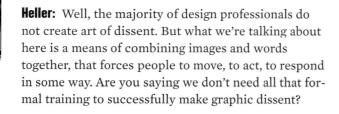

see again or never to think about again. So, you have to be very careful about this kind of violence to the system. On the other hand, some images, even shocking ones, move you not through an empathetic response, but through a tribal one.

Heller: The most effective propagandists always understand that different "markets" require differing nuances. Is this true for the design of dissent?

Glaser: Karl Rove [President Bush's political and public relations advisor] would say you do it one market at a time. Each market responds to something else. So, very often you can't have something that is so generally attractive or compelling that everybody signs on, so you have to say, "Let's look at the 16-to-21-year-olds and communicate there," and then onto the middle-aged people who have something more to lose, and so on. That's how you have to operate if you want to be in the marketing business.

Heller: From what you've seen of the material collected in this book, do you feel that graphic designers are sophisticated enough to know how to approach these markets, or are the designers dealing with their emotions first and the rest comes later?

Glaser: Both. You'll find things in the book that represent both emotional and logical responses. I found the work from Eastern Europe and Bosnia thoughtful about the response they wanted to get. They were also identifying with a certain class of people they seem to know.

It's easier to do that when you are part of the community you're talking to as opposed to being at arms' length of it. I suppose that the most compelling imagery comes out of people who are speaking to their own family—in effect, their brothers, their cousins, their aunts, their uncles—and have that sense that they are a participant in the situation.

Heller: Even in the best-edited collections of socially conscious designed artifacts I see many recurring clichés. The message may be heartfelt, but it comes off as banal because of all the clichés that are used.

Glaser: Stereotypes and clichés are the basic tool of communication, so you have to be careful about how you use them, but you frequently find that they are the most powerful instrument you have in reaching people. You have to re-imagine them. But they are, after all, things that are commonly known, and you are always dealing in the realm of what is already known. I guess what you really mean is that if something is so ordinary and unsurprising in its observation, people simply won't pay any attention to it.

Heller: It becomes wallpaper.

Glaser: And that is the other question of provocation. How can you penetrate people's immunity is always the fundamental question of a designer's work.

Heller: How can a designer improve upon the photographs that leaked out of Abu Ghraib? The TV news and Internet sites showed these horrors minute by minute. In fact, I believe there are so many images on the airwaves that it's hard to focus.

Glaser: Television is different from other things. Objects on television have no reality, regardless of what they are. Whether it's a murder that's being committed before your eyes or a concert from Carnegie Hall, they have equivalent meaning, to some degree. There's something profoundly different about the experience of reading, where the mind is activated, or actually witnessing an event.

Heller: What about the objects of dissent that *you* manufacture? How do you decide what medium to use and what you feel will be the most effective for any particular message? I'm referring specifically to the war in Iraq, which you have protested through your *Nation* magazine button campaign?

Glaser: Campaign buttons are as primitive a form of communication as one can imagine. But if you respect the person wearing them, you tend to respect the message. The button intends to remind people of certain democratic ideals that are perhaps so self-evident that they become invisible. Sometimes, what is most obvious is very difficult to perceive.

Heller: How many ways can a message be presented? And how do you know you are making an impression?

Glaser: The principal problem is the entry point into the cultural bloodstream. When we created the campaign of *Light Up The Sky* during the 2004 presidential election, which occurred when the Republican National Convention was held in New York City, the basic idea was to urge people not to gather in groups, but to go out individually wearing or holding lights. I had originally wanted to post notices around the city, but there was no way I could do it without hiring an illegal sniper, who basically guarantees that he will keep your posters on view in any area of town you want and prevent other people from posting over them. It's totally illegal and totally accepted. Unless you're willing to spend the money that way, you can't even post posters yourself because they will either be ripped down or posted over.

Heller: Or could you rent a billboard?

Black Panther Party Logo
Designer **unknown,** 1967

"Eat" (Poster)
Tomi Ungerer, 1967

Illustration for Le Pave
Ronald Topor, 1968

Heller: Or could you rent a billboard?

Glaser: We tried to buy a billboard during the campaign. It was $100,000 for three weeks. So, you realize that frequently dissent is sort of nominal dissent because the ability to enter into the culture is very costly. Now of course, what you hope for is that these ideas will travel, as they say, virally. That people will catch on, and that the message will quickly circulate. The Internet provides this opportunity, and perhaps, the idea of posting printed objects has become less relevant.

"No More War!" (Poster)
Herb Lubalin, 1968

Heller: There are so many of these protest and advocacy messages that arrive in your email inbox or can be accessed on various websites. There are so many different ways of doing it, too: Flash illustration and animation, JPEGs, and PDFs. Some are engaging because they are funny; others are poignant. Are these having any greater effect than the single button that you wear on your lapel or the poster that you do put up on the side of a building?

Glaser: It's very hard to tell what is effective and what isn't. Certainly, when the Swift Boat guys got on the Internet to attack Democratic candidate John Kerry, they were enormously effective in getting those lies circulated. Then, of course, they knew how to have the media pick up and amplify those ideas. It was a terrifically clever way of using both the Internet and conventional media to basically take a message out to an enormous public. Political activist of an opposing point of view would hope to be equally clever as well, using some combination of buttons and Internet and posters and images and words, to spread the message.

"And babies?" (Poster)
Designer **unknown,**
Photographer **R. L.**
Haeberle, 1970

Heller: Another reason to go back to that question of who do we pay attention to?

Glaser: The problem of the Internet is tremendous information and no judgment. So what I suppose you look for is people or personalities or work that has risen above the noise, and has convinced people of its authenticity. In a democracy, you really need people who rise above the general din and stand for something.

Heller: Given the range of material in this book, do you feel that there are pieces that rise above the din? You can look at them individually and say they're striking, they're clever, or they're compassionate. But, are they all part of a big wave that washes over us? Or is there something there that gives us hope that this can actually work, that minds will be somehow altered by graphic dissent?

Solidarity - Poland '80
(Logo)
Jerzy Janiszewski, 1980

Glaser: I think it does happen. It may not happen the same way all the time. And it would be hard for me to select examples out of this group (I actually don't

want to do it, because it would to some degree parochialize the others.) But my belief is that it does work, that it has an effect, that the results cannot be easily traced, that the consequences of all this material, like everything else in life, is mostly invisible. Actually, I don't think it makes any difference whether you think it works or not. You *have* to do it. It's necessary for dissent to be expressed. It has to be expressed because to protect democracy, it's the only hope we have.

December 2004

Steven Heller, art director of the *New York Times Book Review* and co-chair of the School of Visual Arts MFA Design Program, is the author, co-author, or editor of more than ninety books on graphic design and popular art, including *Merz To Emigre and Beyond: Avant-Garde Magazine Design of the Twentieth Century* (Phaidon Press), *Paul Rand* (Phaidon Press), and *Design Literacy Second Edition* (Allworth Press). He is also the co-author of *Art Against War* (Abbeville Press) and *Angry Graphics* (Gibbs-Smith). He is the recipient of the 1999 AIGA Medal for Lifetime Achievement. He is currently co-writing *Anatomy of Design* with Mirko Ilić for Rockport Publishers, which diagrams the roots and routes of contemporary works of design and typography.

DIRECTORY OF CONTRIBUTORS

A

Majid Abbasi
Did Graphics
10 Palizi Avenue
Tehran 1557974611, Iran
Ph: 98.21.875.02.17
Fax: 98.21.875.02.82
www.didgraphics.com
[189]

Rodney Abbot
352A 14th Street
Brooklyn, NY 11215, USA
Ph: 718.369.6028
[119, 120]

Sean Adams
AdamsMorioka, Inc.
8484 Wilshire Boulevard
Suite 600
Beverly Hills, CA 90211, USA
Ph: 323.966.5990
Fax: 323.966.5994
www.adamsmorioka.com
[126]

Keeno Ahmed
We Saved Our Souls
103 Avenue A #2A
New York, NY 10009, USA
Ph: 917.957.3115
www.wsos.us
[56]

Tahamtan Aminiam
Eshareh
#13 Golazin Alley, Ashkani Street,
Vozara Street
Tehran 1511946811, Iran
Ph: 98.21.888.00.63
Fax: 98.21.877.06.74
www.eshareh.com
[77, 130]

Primo Angeli
Primo Angeli
Via Plinio Il Giovane, 11
06049 Spoleto, Italy
Ph: 39.074340590
[200]

Igor Avzner
Serbia
[81]

B

Aljoša Bagola
PRISTOP
Trubarjeva 79
1000 Ljubljana, Slovenia
Ph: 386.1.2391.200
Fax: 386.1.2391.210
[92]

Susan Barber
Open
180 Varick Street #822
New York, NY 10014, USA
Ph: 212.645.5633
Fax: 212.645.8164
[58, 210]

Jesus Barraza
Tumi's Design
3028 International Boulevard
Oakland, CA 94601, USA
Ph: 510.532.8267
Fax: 510.532.8461
www.tumis.com
[182, 184]

Dana Bartelt
1903 Valence Street
New Orleans, LA 70115, USA
Ph: 504.908.7683
[12, 13, 17]

Beehive Design Collective
3 Elm Street
Machias, ME 04654, USA
Ph: 207.255.6737
www.beehivecollective.org
[193]

Joshua Berger
PLAZM
P.O. Box 2663
Portland, OR 97208, USA
Ph: 503.528.8000
Fax: 503.528.8092
www.plazm.com
[57, 132]

Nicholas Blechman
Knickerbocker Design
416 West 13th Street #309
New York, NY 10014, USA
Ph: 212.229.2831
Fax: 212.229.2756
www.knickerbockerdesign.com
[62, 158, 218]

Jadran Boban
Zeleni Trg 3
Zagreb 10 000, Croatia
Ph: 00.385.169.9244
www.jadranboban.com
[68]

Sanjeev Bothra
Appropriate Design
East 238 Ram Path
Shyamnagar, Jaipur
Rajasthan 302019, India
Ph: 91.141.2292838
[191]

Lisa Boxus
Skart
(In)Extenso
22 Rue Léon Théodor
Bruxelles 1090, Belgium
Ph: 32.2.539.05.96
Fax: 32.2.496.527.176
www.inextenso.be
[48]

Peter Brandt
[231]

Alex Briseño
Florida Freedom Partnership
P.O. Box 144727
Coral Gables, FL 33114, USA
Ph: 305.443.0102
Fax: 305.444.1517
[106]

Steve Brodner
USA
[64]

Cara Brower
Open
180 Varick Street #822
New York, NY 10014, USA
Ph: 212.645.5633
Fax: 212.645.8164
[210]

Susan Brzozowski
And Partners NY
156 5th Avenue #1234
New York, NY 10010, USA
Ph: 212.414.4700
Fax: 212.414.2915
www.andpartnersny.com
[114]

Mauro Bubbico
Via Porta Schiavoney
Montescagudso (MT), Italy
Ph: 0835.208671
Fax: 0835.208671
[109, 111, 129]

Boris Bucàn
Ilica 150
Zagreb, Croatia
Fax: 48.22003
[40–41, 42]

Buenos Aires Stencil Group
Nicaragua 5645
Buenos Aires, Argentina
Ph: 54.11.4772.4051
[181]

Rebecca Bughouse
Bughouse
2268 Hill Drive
Los Angeles, CA 90041, USA
Ph: 323.257.0380
Fax: 323.257.0382
www.bughouse.com
[145]

Jarek Bujny
Ul.Dyw.Wolyunskiej 15 c 15
80-041 Gdansk, Poland
Ph: 48.602.631.544
Fax: 48.586.206.112
[109, 133]

Adrienne Burk
done for myself
12167 Valley Heart Drive
Studio City, CA 91604, USA
Ph: 818.762.6133
Fax: 323.337.0412
[53, 216]

C

Matt Campbell
BBH
7 West 22nd Street, 8th Floor
New York, NY 10010, USA
Ph: 212.812.6641
Fax: 212.989.1122
[154–155]

Ronn Campisi
c/o Frances Jetter Illustration
2211 Broadway #3KN
New York, NY 10024, USA
Ph: 212.580.3720
Fax: 212.877.8528
[118]

Christopher Cardinal
c/o Rebecca Migdal
77 Lefferts Place #2R
Brooklyn, NY 11238, USA
Ph: 718.622.9554
[192]

Fang Chen
Illinois State University
Normal, IL 61761-5620, USA
Ph: 309.532.4616
Fax: 309.438.5625
[85, 128]

Joshua Chen
Chen Design Associates
589 Howard Street #4
San Francisco, CA 94105, USA
Ph: 415.896.5338
Fax: 415.896.5339
www.chendesign.com
[166]

Ivan Chermayeff
Chermayeff & Geismar Inc.
15 East 26th Street
New York, NY 10010, USA
Ph: 212.532.4499
Fax: 212.889.6515
[84]

Nenad Cizl
Mediamix
Kajuhova 12
Maribor 2000, Slovenia
Ph: 386.2.23.50.550
Fax: 386.2.23.50.551
www.mediamix.si
[50, 54]

Sue Coe
USA
[134–135, 203]

Ben Cohen
USA
[195]

Trudy Cole-Zielanski
Trudy Cole-Zielanski Design
629 Moffett Branch Road
Churchville, VA 24421, USA
Ph: 540.568.3488
Fax: 540.568.6598
[113]

Robbie Conal
3522 Meier Street
Los Angeles, CA 90066, USA
Ph: 310.915.0774
[93]

Niko Courtelis
PLAZM
P.O. Box 2663
Portland, OR 97208, USA
Ph: 503.528.8000
Fax: 503.528.8092
www.plazm.com
[132]

G. Dan Covert
Nine2five.net
1902 Folsom Street
San Francisco, CA 94103, USA
Ph: 415.336.5961
www.nine2five.net
[156]

John Creson
Addis Group
2515 9th Street
Berkeley, CA 94710, USA
Ph: 510.704.7500
Fax: 510.704.7501
www.addis.com
[115]

Kimberly Cross
Another Poster for Peace
1712 8th Street
Alameda, CA 94501, USA
Ph: 510.522.2649
[58]

Andrés Mario Ramírez Cuevas
La Máquina del Tiempo
Avenue Universidad 464-A
Narvarte, DF 03600, Mexico
Ph: 52.(55).11.07.77.46
Fax: 52.(55).56.87.41.37
www.lmtgrafica.com
[147, 182, 187]

D

Sam Davidson
c/o Frances Jetter Illustration
2211 Broadway #3KN
New York, NY 10024, USA
Ph: 212.580.3720
Fax: 212.877.8528
[118]

Neels de Coning
Visual Partners Design
Consultancy
42 Pine Walk, Cobham, Surrey,
KT11 2HJ, UK
Ph & Fax: 019.3259.0174
deconing@btconnect.com
[172]

Thomas Dellert-Dellacroix
Studio Utopia
26 Rue le Brun
15013 Paris, France
Ph: 33.1.47.07.7074
Fax: 33.1.47.07.7074
[144, 161]

Agnieszka Dellfina
Studio Utopia
26 Rue le Brun
15013 Paris, France
Ph: 33.1.47.07.7074
Fax: 33.1.47.07.7074
[144, 161]

Sharon DiGiacinto
6741 West Cholla Street
Peoria, AZ 85345, USA
Ph: 623.878.0844
[133]

Diplo **Magazine**
156-158 Gray's Inn Road
London, WC1X 8ED, UK
Ph: 020.7833.9766
[63]

Nikola Djurek
Inside
Varazdinska 3
Zabok 49210, Croatia
Ph: 00.385.49.221.962
Fax: 00.385.49.221.583
[207]

Eric Drooker
P.O. Box 14133
Berkeley, CA 94712, USA
Ph: 510.843.1503
www.drooker.com
[15, 118, 202]

Debra Drovillo
352 A 14th Street
Brooklyn, NY 11215, USA
Ph: 718.369.6028
[119, 120]

Alice Drueding
Scorsone/Drueding
212 Greenwood Avenue
Jenkintown, PA 19046, USA
Ph: 215.572.0782
Fax: 215.572.0782
[79]

Michael Duffy
Duffco
302 Belmont Road
Madison, WI 53714, USA
Ph: 608.249.9255
[69]

E

**Alireza Mostafazadeh
Ebrahimi**
Eshareh
13 Golazin Alley
Ashkani Street, Vozara Street
Tehran 1511946811, Iran
Ph: 9821.888.00.63
Fax: 9821.877.06.74
[80]

Dennis Edge
412 East 9th Street
New York, NY 10009, USA
Ph: 212.420.1110
[57]

Stanley Eisenman
Eisenman Associates
530 Broadway
New York, NY 10012, USA
Ph: 212.941.0550
[72]

Emek
Emek Studios
P.O. Box 801663
Santa Clarita, CA 91380, USA
Ph: 818.415.9309
www.emek.net
[108, 167]

Tan Kien Eng
Ogilvyone Worldwide, Malaysia
Level 11, Menara Milenium
8 JKN Damanlela, Bukit
Damansara
50490 Kuala Lumpur, Malaysia
Ph: 60.327.188.811
Fax: 60.327.106.811
[124, 125]

Matt Erceg
useMEdesign
2446 North West Overton Street
Portland, OR 97210, USA
Ph: 503.222.2878
[153]

Bülent Erkmen
BEK
Cihangir Cad No:18
Cihangir 80060
Istanbul, Turkey
Ph: 90.212.236.27.05
Fax: 90.212.245.28.18
[15]

Matthias Ernstberger
Sagmeister Inc.
222 West 14th Street
New York, NY 10011, USA
Ph: 212.647.1789
Fax: 212.647.1788
www.sagmeister.com
[195]

 F

Ali Ferzat
P.O. Box 36863
Damascus, Syria
Ph & Fax: 963.11.6115255
[191]

Jeff Fisher
Jeff Fisher Logo Motives
P.O. Box 17155
Portland, OR 97217, USA
Ph: 503.283.8673
Fax: 503.283.8995
www.jfisherlogomotives.com
[127]

Mark Fox
Black Dog
409 Sunny Slope Avenue
Petaluma, CA 94952, USA
Ph: 707.769.9082
[87, 167, 170]

**Gabriel Freeman
Javier Freeman
Sonja Freeman**
Un Mundo Fcliz/Λ Happy
World Production
San Andrés 36 2nd P6
28004 Madrid, Spain
Ph: 34.915.943.813
Fax: 34.915.568.123
[51, 94, 105, 171, 209]

G

Tyler Galloway
3922 Wyoming Street
Kansas City, MO 6411, USA
Ph: 816.561.5562
[138, 211]

Ken Garland
71 Albert Street
London, NW1 7LX, UK
Ph: 020.7387.4518
[140, 192]

Tom Geismar
Chermayeff & Geismar Inc.
15 East 26th Street
New York, NY 10010, USA
Ph: 212.532.4499
Fax: 212.889.6515
[84]

Steff Geissbuhler
Chermayeff & Geismar Inc.
15 East 26th Street
New York, NY 10010, USA
Ph: 212.532.4499
Fax: 212.889.6515
[84]

Lisa Gibson
Gibson Design
156 Rising Trail Drive
Middletown, CT 06457, USA
Ph: 860.613.0334
[82]

John Givens
USA
[97, 201]

Milton Glaser
207 East 32nd Street
New York, NY 10016, USA
Ph: 212.889.3161
www.miltonglaser.com
[59, 75, 212, 213]

Kyle Goen
70 Washington Street #257
Brooklyn, NY 11201, USA
Ph: 718.222.8859
[200, 215]

Fermin Gonzalez
600 Northwest W Avenue #8
Miami, FL 33172, USA
Ph: 786.271.2701
[186]

Carole Goodson
Goodson + Yu Design
1823 A Tenth Avenue
Honolulu, HI 96816, USA
Ph: 808.735.6662
Fax: 808.735.9437
[123]

Ellen Gould
c/o Another Poster for Peace
1712 8th Street
Alameda, CA 94501, USA
Ph: 510.522.2649
[74]

Kevin Grady
Gum
91 Main Street #207
Concord, MA 01742, USA
Ph: 978.318.9988
www.gumweb.com
[137]

Copper Greene
480 Broadway, 2nd Floor
New York, NY 10013, USA
[66, 150]

Grupo Arte Callejero Periferia
Peru 1361 #2A
Buenos Aires (1141), Argentina
Ph: 54.11.4300.1844
Fax: 54.11.4300.1844
www.grupoperiferia.com.ar
[193]

Wieslaw Grzegorczyk
Ul. Jagiellonska 32/6
35-025 Rzeszow, Poland
Ph: 48.603.373.085
[78]

Guerrilla Girls, Inc.
532 LaGuardia Place #237
New York, NY 10012, USA
Ph: 310.558.0934
Fax: 310.558.0934
www.guerrillagirls.com
[120, 121]

H

Anur Hadziomerspahic
Ideologija
Merhemica Trg 12/4
Sarajevo, Bosnia and
Herzegovina
Ph: 387.33.945.833
Fax: 387.33.664.947
[34, 35]

Ebrahim Haghighi
E.H.
25 Farahani 9th Street
Asadabadi Avenue
Tehran 14336, Iran
Ph: 98.21.871.10.00
Fax: 98.21.872.46.21
[95]

Samia A. Halaby
P.O. Box 965
New York, NY 10013, USA
Ph: 212.966.3517
[16]

Grzegorz Hańderek
Tatarkiewicza 8 B/2
41-819 Zabrze, Poland
Ph: 48.606.688.604
[171]

Pedram Harby
Setavandyar
11 Entezari Street, Aftab Avenue,
Khoddami Avenue, Vanak
Tehran 19948, Iran
Ph: 98.21.803.26.58
Fax: 98.21.804.65.56
[14, 188]

Lars Harmsen
MAGMA
Bachstraße 43
D-76185 Karlsruhe, Germany
Ph: 49.721.92919.70
Fax: 49.721.92919.80
www.magma-ka.de
[92, 151, 199]

Fons Hickmann
Fons Hickmann M23
Garenhaus
Mariannenplatz 23
D 10997 Berlin, Germany
Ph: 49.30.69518501
Fax: 49.30.6951811
www.fonshickmann.com
[198]

Nancy Hoefig
Addis Group
2515 9th Street
Berkeley, CA 94710, USA
Ph: 510.704.7500
Fax: 510.704.7501
www.addis.com
[116]

Joanne Hom
Addis Group
2515 9th Street
Berkeley, CA 94710, USA
Ph: 510.704.7500
Fax: 510.704.7501
www.addis.com
[119]

Philippe Hulet
2 Rue Du Poteau
1350 Orp-Jauche, Belgium
Ph: 32.479.47.44.04
[48]

I

Hernan Ibañez
Florida Freedom Partnership
P.O. Box 144727
Coral Gables, FL 33114, USA
Ph: 305.443.0102
Fax: 305.444.1517
[106]

Mirko Ilić Corp.
207 East 32nd
New York, NY 10016, USA
Ph: 212.481.9737
Fax: 212.481.7088
www.mirkoilic.com
[43, 54, 64, 127, 217]

J

Daniel Jasper
University of Minnesota Twin
Cities
2405 24th Avenue South
Minneapolis, MN 55406, USA
Ph: 612.724.1744
[71]

Frances Jetter
Frances Jetter Illustration
2211 Broadway #3KN
New York, NY 10024, USA
Ph: 212.580.3720
Fax: 212.877.8528
[118]

Haley Johnson
Haley Johnson Design
3107 East 42nd Street
Minneapolis, MN 55406, USA
Ph: 612.722.8050
Fax: 612.722.5989
www.hjd.com
[217]

K

Boris Kahl
MAGMA
Bachstraße 43
D-76185 Karlsruhe, Germany
Ph: 49.721.92919.70
Fax: 49.721.92919.80
www.magma-ka.de
[92]

Šejla Kamerić
Paromlinska 25
71 000 Sarajevo, Bosnia and
Herzegovina
Ph: 387.61.165.925
Fax: 387.33.209.715
www.sejlakameric.com
[32]

Suada Kapić
c/o Fama International
Grbavicka 41
33000 Sarajevo, Bosnia and
Herzegovina
Ph: 387.33.614.827
Fax: 387.33.614.827
[29, 30–31]

Hjalti Karlsson
Karlssonwilker
536 6th Avenue
New York, NY 10011, USA
Ph: 212.929.8064
Fax: 212.929.8063
www.karlssonwilker.com
[194]

Emir Kasumagić
Bosnia and Herzegovina
[29]

Ethel Kessler
Kessler Design Group, Ltd
6931 Arlington Road
Bethesda, MD 20814, USA
Ph: 301.907.3233
Fax: 301.907.6690
www.kesslerdesigngroup.com
[98]

Garland Kirkpatrick
Helvetica Jones
1301 Marine Street
Santa Monica, CA 90405, USA
Ph: 310.351.3216
www.helveticajones.com
[171]

Kate Kittredge
Open
180 Varick Street #822
New York, NY 10014, USA
Ph: 212.645.5633
Fax: 212.645.8164
[210]

Connie Koch
Hello [NYC]
216 East 6th Street
New York, NY 10003, USA
Ph: 212.253.1042
Fax: 212.253.0849
www.hellonyc.net
[60–61]

Judy Kohn
Old Glory Condoms
P.O. Box 819
Provincetown, MA 02657, USA
Ph: 508.487.3684
Fax: 508.487.1930
[128]

Tomato Košir
Britof 141
Kranj, S1-4000, Slovenia
Ph: 386.41.260.979
[99, 152]

Nikola Kostandinović
Nik-Press
Kumodraska 99/29
11000 Beograd, Serbia and
Montenegro
Ph: 38111.2461241
[49]

Cedomir Kostovic
901 East Loren Street
Springfield, MO 65807, USA
Ph: 417.831.6007
Fax: 417.836.6117
[38, 39, 86]

Reem Kotob
Nissan Building
Paris Avenue Street
Jal El Bahr-Beirut, Lebanon
Ph: 961.3.841.603
[151]

Robert Križmančič
PRISTOP
Trubarjeva 79
1000 Ljubljana, Slovenia
Ph: 386.1.2391.200
Fax: 386.1.2391.210
[214]

Dejan Kršić
Arkzin
B. Trenka 4
Zagreb HR-1000, Croatia
Ph: 3851.49.22.478
Fax: 3851.49.22.478
[7, 44, 45, 141, 204–205]

Kohn Kruikshank
Old Glory Condoms
P.O. Box 819
Provincetown, MA 02657, USA
Ph: 508.487.3684
Fax: 508.487.1930
[128]

Boris Kuk
Božesačuvaj
Podgorjoa 3
10000 Zagreb, Croatia
Ph: 00.385.91.2296.117
Fax: 00.385.1.3631.897
[45, 157]

Malik "Kula" Kulenovic
Sarajevo
[28]

Peter Kuper
235 West 102nd Street
New York, NY 10025, USA
Ph: 212.932.1722
Fax: 212.531.4412
[53, 64, 162, 217, 218]

L

Jim Lasser
Planet Propaganda
605 Williamson Street
Madison, WI 53703, USA
Ph: 608.256.000
Fax: 608.256.1975
[65]

Yossi Lemel
3 Hamelakha Street
Tel Aviv 67215, Israel
Ph: 972.3.7616707
Fax: 972.3.7616701
www.lemel.co.il
[21, 22, 23, 24, 25, 33, 76]

Saša Dušan Leskovar
PRISTOP
Trubarjeva 79
1000 Ljubljana, Slovenia
Ph: 386.1.2391.200
Fax: 386.1.2391.210
[92]

Josh Levine
Neutron, LLC
444 De Haro Street
San Francisco, CA 84105, USA
Ph: 415.626.9700
Fax: 415.626.9711
www.neutronllc.com
[57]

Sheila Levrant de Bretteville
Open
180 Varick Street #822
New York, NY 10014, USA
Ph: 212.645.5633
Fax: 212.645.8164
[58]

Andrew Lewis
Andrew Lewis Design
7237 Norman Lane
Brentwood Bay, BC V8M 1C6,
Canada
Ph: 250.652.9581
Fax: 250.652.9576
www.alewisdesign.com
[212]

Rico Lins
Rico Lins + Studio
Rua Campevas, 617
São Paulo SP 05016.010, Brazil
Ph: 55.11.3675.3507
www.ricolins.com
[1, 99]

Boris Ljubicic
Studio International
B4 Conjiceva 43
Zagreb HR-10000, Croatia
Ph: 00.385.13.760.171
Fax: 00.385.13.760.172
www.studio-international.com
[43, 44]

Christopher Loch
Contempl8 T-Shirts
6145 15th Avenue South
Minneapolis, MN 55423, USA
Ph: 612.735.3494
Fax: 508.302.5345
www.contempl8.net
[56]

Jeff Louviere
Louviere + Vanessa
732 Mazant Street
New Orleans, LA 70117, USA
Ph: 504.940.5498
www.louviereandvanessa.com
[110, 165]

Michael Lutz
Gruppe 10
Bachstraße 43
D-76185 Karlsruhe, Germany
Ph: 49.721.92919.70
Fax: 49.721.92919.80
www.magma-ka.de
[151, 199]

M

Michael Mabry
Michael Mabry Design
1500 Park Avenue #112
Emeryville, CA 94608, USA
Ph: 510.985.0750
Fax: 510.985.0753
www.michaelmabry.com
[80, 158]

Josh MacPhee
Justseeds
P.O. Box 476971
Chicago, IL 60647, USA
Ph: 773.342.8251
[75]

Lisa Mangano
352 A 14th Street
Brooklyn, NY 11215, USA
Ph: 718.369.6028
[119, 120]

Chaz Maviyane-Davies
247 Garden Street, Apt. 10
Cambridge, MA 02138, USA
Ph: 617.547.5292
[67, 90–91, 117, 146, 176, 177]

Pete McCracken
PLAZM
P.O. Box 2663
Portland, OR 97208, USA
Ph: 503.528.8000
Fax: 503.528.8092
www.plazm.com
[132]

Rebecca Migdal
77 Lefferts Place #2R
Brooklyn, NY 11238, USA
Ph: 718.622.9554
[192]

Joe Miller
Joe Miller's Company
3080 Olcott Street #210A
Santa Clara, CA 95054, USA
Ph: 408.988.2924
Fax: 408.727.9941
[55]

Alexandra Min
352A 14th Street
Brooklyn, NY 11215, USA
Ph: 718.369.6028
[119, 120]

Naomi Mizusaki
Knickerbocker Design
416 West 13th Street #309
New York, NY 10014, USA
Ph: 212.229.2831
Fax: 212.229.2756
www.knickerbockerdesign.com
[62]

Jaka Modic
PRISTOP
Trubarjeva 79
1000 Ljubljana, Slovenia
Ph: 386.1.2391.200
Fax: 386.1.2391.210
[79]

Enrique Mosqueda
PLAZM
P.O. Box 2663
Portland, OR 97208, USA
Ph: 503.528.8000
Fax: 503.528.8092
www.plazm.com
[132]

Lejla Mulabegovic
Trio Sarajevo
Branislava Auraeva 4
71000 Sarajevo, Bosnia and
Herzegovina
Ph: 387.33.253.903
Fax: 387.33.253.903
[26–27, 33, 36–37]

N

Marty Neumeier
Neutron, LLC
444 De Haro Street
San Francisco, CA 84105, USA
Ph: 415.626.9700
Fax: 415.626.9711
www.neutronllc.com
[57, 73]

New Collectivism
Golo Brdo 82
1215 Medvode, Slovenia
Ph: 386.136.18341
Fax: 386.136.18340
[4, 5, 6]

Miran Norderland
FAMA International
Grbavicka 41
33 000 Sarajevo, Bosnia and
Herzegovina
Ph: 387.33.619.8.27
Fax: 387.33.619.827
www.famainternational.com
[29]

Ranko Novak
DesigNovak
Mislejeva 3
1000 Ljubljana, Slovenia
Ph: 00386.1.43.700.63
Fax: 00386.1.43.700.63
[43]

Jan Nuckowski
Self-Made
OS. Dywizjonv 303, 14-15
Krakow 21-872, Poland
Ph: 48.126.47.5959
[99]

O

Ahmet Ogut
Diybakir Sanat Merkezi Diyar
Galeria
Alisveris Merkezi #9
Dagkapi, Diyarbakir 21100,
Turkey
Ph: 00.90.505.567.70.54
Fax: 00.90.412.252.10.11
[173]

Travis Olson
Carmichael Lynch Thorburn
800 Hennepin Avenue
Minneapolis, MN 55403, USA
Ph: 612.375.8231
[218]

Anotoliy Omelchenko
335 93rd Street
Brooklyn, NY 11209, USA
Ph: 646.250.9405
Fax: 718.748.9406
[131, 175]

Istvan Orosz
Hungary
[2, 3]

Sener Ozmen
Diybakir Sanat Merkezi Diyar
Galeria
Alisveris Merkezi #9
Dagkapi, Diyarbakir 21100,
Turkey
Ph: 00.90.505.567.70.54
Fax: 00.90.412.252.10.11
[173]

P

Scott Palmer
We Saved Our Souls
103 Avenue A #2A
New York, NY 10009, USA
Ph: 917.957.3115
www.wsos.us
[56]

Adriana Parcero
A-Parcero Studio
1800 North New Hampshire
Avenue #222
Los Angeles, CA 90027, USA
Ph: 323.252.8784
Fax: 323.668.1533
[107]

Wishmini Perera
329 10th Street
San Francisco, CA 94103, USA
Ph: 415.533.2344
[117]

Emilio Petersen
Nicaragua 5645 20 "5"
Buenos Aires, Argentina
Ph: 54.11.4772.4051
[178–179, 180, 181]

Dušan Petričić
182 Woodcrest Avenue
Toronto M4J 3A7, Canada
Ph: 416.778.1987
Fax: 416.778.1943
[125]

Woody Pirtle
Pentagram Design
204 5th Avenue
New York, NY 10010, USA
Ph: 212.683.7000
Fax: 212.532.0181
www.pentagram.com
[100, 101, 102–103, 159]

Péter Pócs
Poster'V Ltd.
Tamási Áron utca 18/B
Budapest 1124, Hungary
Ph: 361.225.0779
Fax: 361.225.0780
www.posters.hu
[8, 9, 10, 11, 149]

Tom Porostocky
USA
[219]

Q

Qian Qian
3515 East Lombard
#A201
Springfield, MO 65809, USA
Ph: 417.848.0295
[151]

R

Erena Rae
Thistlewood Press
7th Avenue #126
Highland Park, NJ 08904-2932,
USA
Ph: 732.339.1346
[211]

Rebecca Rapp
New Orleans, LA, USA
[12]

Andrea Rauch
Rauch Design
Italy
Ph: 39.055.965489
Fax: 39.055.965505
www.rauchdesign.com
[46, 193, 197]

Dan Reisinger
Studio Reisinger
3 Rama Street
53320 Givatayim, Israel
Ph: 972.3.5714982
Fax: 972.3.5711695
www.visualarts.co.il/english
[1, 22]

James Riseborough
c/o Sagmeister Inc.
222 West 14th Street
New York, NY 10011, USA
Ph: 212.647.1789
Fax: 212.647.1788
www.sagmeister.com
[62, 194, 195]

Favianna Rodríguez
Tumi's Design
3028 International Boulevard
Oakland, CA 94601, USA
Ph: 510.532.8267
Fax: 510.532.8461
[142]

Renato Aranda Rodríguez
Renato Aranda Studio
Cumbres de Maltrata 158-2
Navarte, DF 03020, Mexico
[55, 97]

David Rojas
Av. Universidad 1953
Mexico City, DF 04340, Mexico
Ph: 52.55.56.16.39.38
[183]

Charlie Ross
Carmichael Lynch Thorburn
800 Hennepin Avenue
Minneapolis, MN 55403, USA
Ph: 612.334.6000
www.clthorburn.com
[164]

Erika Rothenberg
2020 Nichols Canyon
Los Angeles, CA 90046, USA
Ph: 310.558.0934
Fax: 310.558.0934
[131]

Dejan Dragosavac Rutta
Arkzin
B. Trenka 4
Zagreb HR-1000, Croatia
Ph: 3851.49.22.478
Fax: 3851.49.22.478
[44, 141, 204–205]

S

Nour Saab
Nissan Building
Paris Avenue Street
Jal El Bahr-Beirut, Lebanon
Ph: 961.3.841.603
[151]

Margarita Sada
La Muñequitas Contraatacan
Av. Universidad 464-A
Narvarte, DF 03600, Mexico
Ph: 52.(55).11.07.77.46
Fax: 52.(55).56.87.41.37
[112, 118]

Mehdi Saeedi
Graphic Studio Mehdi Saeedi
No. 275 Orkide Gharbi
Alley.Shahrak Golestan
St. 35 Metry Esteghlal. Ave
Hengam SQ. Resalat
Tehran 16879-83711, Iran
Ph: 98.21.736.57.70
www.mehdisaeedi.com
[83]

Leonel Sagahón
La Máquina del Tiempo
Avenue Universidad 464-A
Narvarte, DF 03600, Mexico
Ph: 52 (55) 11.07.77.46
Fax: 52 (55) 56.87.41.37
www.lmtgrafica.com
[182, 185]

Stefan Sagmeister
Sagmeister Inc.
222 West 14th Street
New York, NY 10011, USA
Ph: 212.647.1789
Fax: 212.647.1788
www.sagmeister.com
[62, 194, 195]

Mike Salisbury LLC
P.O. Box 2309
Venice, CA 90291, USA
Ph: 310.392.8779
Fax: 310.392.9488
[78]

David Sarhandi
Puerto Real 67-9
Colonia Condesa
Mexico City, Mexico
Ph: 52.55.52.86.07.50
Fax: 52.55.52.86.07.50
[26–27]

Bijan Sayfouri
Bijan Sayfouri Studio
109 Ebn-e sina Street #4
Yousefabad, Tehran 1434654355,
Iran
Ph: 98.21.806.32.77
Fax: 98.21.806.32.77
[190, 191]

Noah Scalin
ALR Design
2701 Edgewood Avenue
Richmond, VA 23220, USA
Ph: 804.321.6677
Fax: 804.321.6677
www.alrdesign.com
[58]

Paula Scher
Pentagram Design
204 5th Avenue
New York, NY 10010, USA
Ph: 212.683.7000
Fax: 212.532.0181
www.pentagram.com
[206]

Sandra Scher
Juice Creative Group
289 President Street
Apartment #2
Brooklyn, NY 11231, USA
Ph: 718.852.9330
[136, 138, 139]

David Schimmel
And Partners NY
156 5th Avenue #1234
New York, NY 10010, USA
Ph: 212.414.4700
Fax: 212.414.2915
www.andpartnersny.com
[114]

Monica Schlaug
Addis Group
2515 9th Street
Berkeley, CA 94710, USA
Ph: 510.704.7500
Fax: 510.704.7501
www.addis.com
[115, 116]

Joe Scorsone
Scorsone/Drueding
212 Greenwood Avenue
Jenkintown, PA 19046, USA
Ph: 215.572.0782
Fax: 215.572.0782
[79]

Louise Scovell
352 A 14th Street
Brooklyn, NY 11215, USA
Ph: 718.369.6028
[119, 120]

Bojan Senjur
PRISTOP
Trubarjeva 79
1000 Ljubljana, Slovenia
Ph: 386.1.2391.200
Fax: 386.1.2391.210
[79]

Stanislav Sharp
Art Group FIA
Hilandarska 4
11000 Belgrade, Serbia and
Montenegro
Ph: 381.11.3247.355
Fax: 381.11.3247.355
[47, 137]

Lisa Shoglow
352 A 14th Street
Brooklyn, NY 11215, USA
Ph: 718.369.6028
[119, 120]

Tom Sieu
Tom Sieu Design
822 Peralta Avenue
San Francisco, CA 94110, USA
Ph: 415.722.4216
[97, 201]

Araba Simpson
120 Manhattan Ave #4A
New York, NY 10025, USA
Ph: 917.520.7462
[96]

Surinder Singh
c/o Orange Juice Design
461 Berea Road
Durban 4001, South Africa
Ph: 27.31.2771860
Fax: 27.31.2771870
[89]

Sonja Smith
316 North Ridgewood Place
Los Angeles, CA 90004, USA
Ph: 818.238.6253
Fax: 818.562.9235
[163]

Lanny Sommese
Sommese Design
100 Rose Drive
Port Matilda, PA 16870, USA
Ph: 814.353.1951
Fax: 814.865.1158
[105]

James Song
269 5th Avenue #1R
San Francisco, CA 94118, USA
Ph: 415.971.0351
[208]

May L. Sorum
7542 16th Avenue North West
Seattle, WA 98117, USA
Ph: 206.784.6874
[52]

Max Spector
Chen Design Associates
589 Howard Street #4
San Francisco, CA 94105, USA
Ph: 415.896.5338
Fax: 415.896.5339
www.chendesign.com
[166]

Vladan Srdić
Thesign
Kotnikova 34
1000 Yubyana, Slovenia
Ph: 386.31.847.261
www.thedesign.org.uk
[149, 160]

Damion Steele
718 East 9th Street
Mishawaka, IN 46544, USA
Ph: 574.255.6527
[145]

Slavimir Stojanović
FUTRO
Jesenkova 2
SI-1000 Ljubljana, Slovenia
Ph: 386.41.320597
[98]

Scott Stowell
Open
180 Varick Street #822
New York, NY 10014, USA
Ph: 212.645.5633
Fax: 212.645.8164
[58, 126, 210]

Herb Stratford
Kerry Stratford
308 East 2nd Street
Tucson, AZ 85705, USA
Ph: 520.628.1683
Fax: 520.628.1990
[168]

Richard Strydom
P.O. Box 20808
Noordbrug 2522, South Africa
Ph: 27.82.575.0923
Fax: 27.18.299.1516
[148]

Ward Sutton
Sutton Impact Studio
799 Greenwich Street #4-5
New York, NY 10014, USA
Ph: 212.924.4992
[143, 162, 218]

T

David Tartakover
Tartakover Design
34 Chelouche Street
Tel Aviv 65149, Israel
Ph: 972.3.5173745
Fax: 972.3.5177678
[18, 19, 20, 21, 149]

Ashton Taylor
AdamsMorioka, Inc.
8484 Wilshire Boulevard
Suite 600
Beverly Hills, CA 90211, USA
Ph: 323.966.5990
Fax: 323.966.5994
www.adamsmorioka.com
[126]

Theresa Tsang Teng
Ogilvyone Worldwide, Malaysia
Level 11, Menara Milenium
8 JKN Damanlela, Bukit
Damansara
50490 Kuala Lumpur, Malaysia
Ph: 60.327.188.811
Fax: 60.327.106.811
[122, 124]

Valerie Thai
11500 Blundell
Richmond, BC V64 113, Canada
Ph: 604.738.7690
[163]

Mr. Tharp
Tharp Did It
50 University Avenue #21
Los Gatos, CA 95030, USA
Ph: 408.354.6726
Fax: 408.354.1450
[83]

Patrick Thomas
Studio laVista
Ptge de Masoliver 25-27
08005 Barcelona, Spain
Ph: 34.933.208.114
www.lavistadesign.com
[74]

Seth Tobocman
c/o Rebecca Migdal
77 Lefferts Place #2R
Brooklyn, NY 11238, USA
Ph: 718.622.9554
[192]

Jennifer Tolo
Chen Design Associates
589 Howard Street #4
San Francisco, CA 94105, USA
Ph: 415.896.5338
Fax: 415.896.5339
www.chengdesign.com
[166]

Toni Tomašek
Mediamix
Kajuhova 12
Maribor 2000, Slovenia
Ph: 386.2.23.50.550
Fax: 386.2.23.50.551
www.mediamix.si
[50, 54]

Trio Sarajevo
Branislava Auraeva 4
71000 Sarajevo, Bosnia and
Herzegovina
Ph: 387.33.253.903
Fax: 387.33.253.903
[26–27, 33, 36–37]

U

Albino Uršić
Božesačuvaj
Podgorjoa 3
10000 Zagreb, Croatia
Ph: 00.385.91.2296.117
Fax: 00.385.1.3631.897
[45, 157]

V

Yarom Vardimdon
Yarom Vardimdon Design
87 Shlomo Hamelech Street
Tel Aviv 64512, Israel
Ph: 972.3.5239361.5233748
Fax: 972.3.5245268
[96, 208]

Yoost Veerkanp
c/o Orange Juice Design
461 Berea Road
Durban 4001, South Africa
Ph: 27.31.2771860
Fax: 27.31.2771870
[89]

Samuli Viitasaari
Studio Ilpo Okkonen Oy
Rautatienkatu 16 D 68
F1-90100 Oulu, Finland
Ph: 358.40.722.32.64
Fax: 358.8.815.0222
[74]

Jugoslav Vlahović
NIN
Marsala Birjuzova 27
11000 Belgrade, Serbia and
Montenegro
Ph: 381.11.626.903
Fax: 381.11.3373.213
[80]

Jelena Vranic
FAMA International
Grbavicka 41
33 000 Sarajevo, Bosnia and
Herzegovina
Ph: 387.33.619.8.27
Fax: 387.33.619.827
www.famainternational.com
[29]

W

Kevin Wade
Planet Propaganda
605 Williamson Street
Madison, WI 53703, USA
Ph: 608.256.000
Fax: 608.256.1975
[65]

Lutz Wahler
Gruppe 10
Bachstraße 43
D-76185 Karlsruhe, Germany
Ph: 49.721.92919.70
Fax: 49.721.92919.80
www.magma-ka.de
[151, 199]

Garth Walker
Orange Juice Design
461 Berea Road
Durban 4001, South Africa
Ph: 27.31.2771860
Fax: 27.31.2771870
[87, 140]

Ginny Warren
Invent
19 Forest Street #21
Cambridge, MA 02140, USA
Ph: 617.868.4192
Fax: 617.423.5920
[214]

Ulrich Weiß
MAGMA
Bachstraße 43
D-76185 Karlsruhe, Germany
Ph: 49.721.92919.70
Fax: 49.721.92919.80
www.magma-ka.de
[92, 151, 199]

Carrie Whitney
c/o Peter Kuper
235 West 102nd Street
New York, NY 10025, USA
Ph: 212.932.1722
Fax: 212.531.4412
[53]

Samantha Wilson
c/o Rebecca Migdal
77 Lefferts Place #2R
Brooklyn, NY 11238, USA
Ph: 718.622.9554
[192]

Ewa Wlostowska
Ul. Jana Pawla II 23B/9
Brzeg 49-300, Poland
[174]

Y

John Yates
Stealworks
2830 Encinal Avenue
Alameda, CA 94501, USA
Ph: 510.337.9511
www.stealworks.com
[70, 169, 196]

Tadanori Yokoo
5-22-2 Seijo Setagaya-ku
Tokyo 157-0066, Japan
Ph: 81.3.3482.2826
Fax: 81.3.3482.2451
[104]

Daniel Young
Daniel Young Studio
207 East 32nd Street
New York, NY 10016, USA
Ph: 212.696.1264
Fax: 212.213.4072
[170, 217]

Shi-Zhe Yung
Adbusters Media Foundation
1243 West 7th Avenue
Vancouver, BC V6H 1B7, Canada
Ph: 604.736.9401
Fax: 604.737.6021
[143]

Z

Mateja D. Zavrl
PRISTOP
Trubarjeva 79
1000 Ljubljana, Slovenia
Ph: 386.1.2391.200
Fax: 386.1.2391.210
[214]

Lloyd Ziff
Mike Salisbury LLC
P.O. Box 2309
Venice, CA 90291, USA
Ph: 310.392.8779
Fax: 310.392.9488
[78]

ACKNOWLDGEMENTS

JESSI ARRINGTON • AMY AXLER
SIMONA BARTA • DANA BARTELT
AMIR BERBIĆ • TERRENCE BROWN
ASJA DUPANOVIĆ • EKREM DUPANOVIĆ
STEVEN HELLER • ALEXANDRA KANE
ČEDOMIR KOSTOVIĆ • DEJAN KRŠIĆ
JEE-EUN LEE • MARIJA MILJKOVIĆ
DAOUD SARHANDI • ARABA SIMPSON
STAFF OF TIPOGRAFICA MAGAZINE
SCHOOL OF VISUAL ARTS • GARTH WALKER
LAETITIA WOLFF • HELEN WU

First published
in the United States of America by
Rockport Publishers, Inc.
33 Commercial Street
Gloucester, Massachusetts 01930-5089

Telephone: (978) 282-9590
Fax: (978) 283-2742
www.rockpub.com

Library of Congress
Cataloging-in-Publication available

ISBN-13: 978-1-59253-307-7
ISBN-10: 1-59253-307-8

10 9 8 7 6 5 4 3 2

Cover Design: Milton Glaser and Mirko Ilić
Book Design: Mirko Ilić Corp., NY
Project Coordinator: Simona Barta

Library of Congress Prints and Photographs
Division, 226 (third); 227 (bottom); 229

DEDICATION

MARTIN LUTHER KING, JR.

CONTENTS